The Tragedie of
Hamlet
Prince of Denmark

By Edward de Vere

Art:
Portrait of Edward de Vere
17th Earl of Oxford (1550-1604)

This edition produced by
Verus Publishing

V | P

www.verusbooks.com

Copyright 2020 Verus Publishing
This book, with the exception of the text of the play itself,
remains the copyrighted property of the publisher and may not
be duplicated or redistributed in whole or in part without
express permission.

ISBN: 978-1-951267-24-7
Imprint / Publisher: Verus Publishing

This book is dedicated to
Alexander Waugh
whose passionate scholarship
inspired this series.

The Author

Edward de Vere, 17th Earl of Oxford

Biography and Bibliography
After the Play

A Preverse

Drone on ye learned scholars of the day
As to with whom the words ahead the credit lay.
For our part though can be no further doubt
That the author of these words has been found out
To be a person lordly and refined
On whom the light of wit so boldly shined
That to keep this wit from tearing in the fray
He gave another, lesser wit his say.

Now let the least of wits
That writes these paltry lines
Yield to him whose peerless name
Should be with reverence spake.
Let this name be not of history's misassigns
Whose pen and verse have made the earth to shake.

The Tragedie of
Hamlet
Prince of Denmark

By Edward de Vere

The Main Characters

Hamlet - Prince of Denmark - son to the late King Hamlet and nephew to the present King Claudius.

Claudius - King of Denmark, elected to the throne after the death of his brother, King Hamlet.

Gertrude - Queen of Denmark, and King Hamlet's widow, now married to Claudius and mother to Hamlet

The Ghost - Of Hamlet's father, the late King Hamlet

Polonius - Claudius' chief counsellor and father of Ophelia and Laertes.

Laertes - Son of Polonius

Ophelia - Daughter of Polonius, and Laertes's sister

Horatio - Friend of Hamlet

Rosencrantz and Guildenstern - Schoolmates and friends of Hamlet

ACT 1

SCENE I

Elsinore. A platform before the castle. FRANCISCO at his post. Enter to him BERNARDO

BERNARDO
Who's there?
FRANCISCO
Nay, answer me: stand, and unfold yourself.
BERNARDO
Long live the king!
FRANCISCO
Bernardo?
BERNARDO
He.
FRANCISCO
You come most carefully upon your hour.
BERNARDO
'Tis now struck twelve; get thee to bed, Francisco.
FRANCISCO
For this relief much thanks: 'tis bitter cold,
And I am sick at heart.
BERNARDO
Have you had quiet guard?
FRANCISCO
Not a mouse stirring.
BERNARDO
Well, good night.
If you do meet Horatio and Marcellus,
The rivals of my watch, bid them make haste.
FRANCISCO
I think I hear them. Stand, ho! Who's there?

The Tragedie of Hamlet — Act I

Enter HORATIO and MARCELLUS

HORATIO
  Friends to this ground.
MARCELLUS
  And liegemen to the Dane.
FRANCISCO
  Give you good night.
MARCELLUS
  O, farewell, honest soldier:
  Who hath relieved you?
FRANCISCO
  Bernardo has my place.
  Give you good night.

Exit

MARCELLUS
  Holla! Bernardo!
BERNARDO
  Say,
  What, is Horatio there?
HORATIO
  A piece of him.
BERNARDO
  Welcome, Horatio: welcome, good Marcellus.
MARCELLUS
  What, has this thing appear'd again to-night?
BERNARDO
  I have seen nothing.
MARCELLUS
  Horatio says 'tis but our fantasy,
  And will not let belief take hold of him
  Touching this dreaded sight, twice seen of us:

Therefore I have entreated him along
With us to watch the minutes of this night;
That if again this apparition come,
He may approve our eyes and speak to it.
HORATIO
Tush, tush, 'twill not appear.
BERNARDO
Sit down awhile;
And let us once again assail your ears,
That are so fortified against our story
What we have two nights seen.
HORATIO
Well, sit we down,
And let us hear Bernardo speak of this.
BERNARDO
Last night of all,
When yond same star that's westward from the pole
Had made his course to illume that part of heaven
Where now it burns, Marcellus and myself,
The bell then beating one,--

Enter Ghost

MARCELLUS
Peace, break thee off; look, where it comes again!
BERNARDO
In the same figure, like the king that's dead.
MARCELLUS
Thou art a scholar; speak to it, Horatio.
BERNARDO
Looks it not like the king? mark it, Horatio.
HORATIO
Most like: it harrows me with fear and wonder.
BERNARDO
It would be spoke to.

MARCELLUS
    Question it, Horatio.
HORATIO
    What art thou that usurp'st this time of night,
    Together with that fair and warlike form
    In which the majesty of buried Denmark
    Did sometimes march? by heaven I charge thee, speak!
MARCELLUS
    It is offended.
BERNARDO
    See, it stalks away!
HORATIO
    Stay! speak, speak! I charge thee, speak!

Exit Ghost

MARCELLUS
    'Tis gone, and will not answer.
BERNARDO
    How now, Horatio! you tremble and look pale:
    Is not this something more than fantasy?
    What think you on't?
HORATIO
    Before my God, I might not this believe
    Without the sensible and true avouch
    Of mine own eyes.
MARCELLUS
    Is it not like the king?
HORATIO
    As thou art to thyself:
    Such was the very armour he had on
    When he the ambitious Norway combated;
    So frown'd he once, when, in an angry parle,
    He smote the sledded Polacks on the ice.
    'Tis strange.

MARCELLUS

Thus twice before, and jump at this dead hour,
With martial stalk hath he gone by our watch.

HORATIO

In what particular thought to work I know not;
But in the gross and scope of my opinion,
This bodes some strange eruption to our state.

MARCELLUS

Good now, sit down, and tell me, he that knows,
Why this same strict and most observant watch
So nightly toils the subject of the land,
And why such daily cast of brazen cannon,
And foreign mart for implements of war;
Why such impress of shipwrights, whose sore task
Does not divide the Sunday from the week;
What might be toward, that this sweaty haste
Doth make the night joint-labourer with the day:
Who is't that can inform me?

HORATIO

That can I;
At least, the whisper goes so. Our last king,
Whose image even but now appear'd to us,
Was, as you know, by Fortinbras of Norway,
Thereto prick'd on by a most emulate pride,
Dared to the combat; in which our valiant Hamlet--
For so this side of our known world esteem'd him--
Did slay this Fortinbras; who by a seal'd compact,
Well ratified by law and heraldry,
Did forfeit, with his life, all those his lands
Which he stood seized of, to the conqueror:
Against the which, a moiety competent
Was gaged by our king; which had return'd
To the inheritance of Fortinbras,
Had he been vanquisher; as, by the same covenant,

And carriage of the article design'd,
His fell to Hamlet. Now, sir, young Fortinbras,
Of unimproved mettle hot and full,
Hath in the skirts of Norway here and there
Shark'd up a list of lawless resolutes,
For food and diet, to some enterprise
That hath a stomach in't; which is no other--
As it doth well appear unto our state--
But to recover of us, by strong hand
And terms compulsatory, those foresaid lands
So by his father lost: and this, I take it,
Is the main motive of our preparations,
The source of this our watch and the chief head
Of this post-haste and romage in the land.

BERNARDO

I think it be no other but e'en so:
Well may it sort that this portentous figure
Comes armed through our watch; so like the king
That was and is the question of these wars.

HORATIO

A mote it is to trouble the mind's eye.
In the most high and palmy state of Rome,
A little ere the mightiest Julius fell,
The graves stood tenantless and the sheeted dead
Did squeak and gibber in the Roman streets:
As stars with trains of fire and dews of blood,
Disasters in the sun; and the moist star
Upon whose influence Neptune's empire stands
Was sick almost to doomsday with eclipse:
And even the like precurse of fierce events,
As harbingers preceding still the fates
And prologue to the omen coming on,
Have heaven and earth together demonstrated
Unto our climatures and countrymen.--

But soft, behold! lo, where it comes again!

Re-enter Ghost

I'll cross it, though it blast me. Stay, illusion!
If thou hast any sound, or use of voice,
Speak to me:
If there be any good thing to be done,
That may to thee do ease and grace to me,
Speak to me:

Cock crows

If thou art privy to thy country's fate,
Which, happily, foreknowing may avoid, O, speak!
Or if thou hast uphoarded in thy life
Extorted treasure in the womb of earth,
For which, they say, you spirits oft walk in death,
Speak of it: stay, and speak! Stop it, Marcellus.
MARCELLUS
  Shall I strike at it with my partisan?
HORATIO
  Do, if it will not stand.
BERNARDO
  'Tis here!
HORATIO
  'Tis here!
MARCELLUS
  'Tis gone!

Exit Ghost

  We do it wrong, being so majestical,
  To offer it the show of violence;
  For it is, as the air, invulnerable,
  And our vain blows malicious mockery.
BERNARDO

It was about to speak, when the cock crew.

HORATIO

And then it started like a guilty thing
Upon a fearful summons. I have heard,
The cock, that is the trumpet to the morn,
Doth with his lofty and shrill-sounding throat
Awake the god of day; and, at his warning,
Whether in sea or fire, in earth or air,
The extravagant and erring spirit hies
To his confine: and of the truth herein
This present object made probation.

MARCELLUS

It faded on the crowing of the cock.
Some say that ever 'gainst that season comes
Wherein our Saviour's birth is celebrated,
The bird of dawning singeth all night long:
And then, they say, no spirit dares stir abroad;
The nights are wholesome; then no planets strike,
No fairy takes, nor witch hath power to charm,
So hallow'd and so gracious is the time.

HORATIO

So have I heard and do in part believe it.
But, look, the morn, in russet mantle clad,
Walks o'er the dew of yon high eastward hill:
Break we our watch up; and by my advice,
Let us impart what we have seen to-night
Unto young Hamlet; for, upon my life,
This spirit, dumb to us, will speak to him.
Do you consent we shall acquaint him with it,
As needful in our loves, fitting our duty?

MARCELLUS

Let's do't, I pray; and I this morning know
Where we shall find him most conveniently.

Exeunt

SCENE II.

A room of state in the castle.

Enter KING CLAUDIUS, QUEEN GERTRUDE, HAMLET, POLONIUS, LAERTES, VOLTIMAND, CORNELIUS, Lords, and Attendants

KING CLAUDIUS

Though yet of Hamlet our dear brother's death
The memory be green, and that it us befitted
To bear our hearts in grief and our whole kingdom
To be contracted in one brow of woe,
Yet so far hath discretion fought with nature
That we with wisest sorrow think on him,
Together with remembrance of ourselves.
Therefore our sometime sister, now our queen,
The imperial jointress to this warlike state,
Have we, as 'twere with a defeated joy,--
With an auspicious and a dropping eye,
With mirth in funeral and with dirge in marriage,
In equal scale weighing delight and dole,--
Taken to wife: nor have we herein barr'd
Your better wisdoms, which have freely gone
With this affair along. For all, our thanks.
Now follows, that you know, young Fortinbras,
Holding a weak supposal of our worth,
Or thinking by our late dear brother's death
Our state to be disjoint and out of frame,
Colleagued with the dream of his advantage,
He hath not fail'd to pester us with message,
Importing the surrender of those lands
Lost by his father, with all bonds of law,
To our most valiant brother. So much for him.

Now for ourself and for this time of meeting:
Thus much the business is: we have here writ
To Norway, uncle of young Fortinbras,--
Who, impotent and bed-rid, scarcely hears
Of this his nephew's purpose,--to suppress
His further gait herein; in that the levies,
The lists and full proportions, are all made
Out of his subject: and we here dispatch
You, good Cornelius, and you, Voltimand,
For bearers of this greeting to old Norway;
Giving to you no further personal power
To business with the king, more than the scope
Of these delated articles allow.
Farewell, and let your haste commend your duty.

CORNELIUS VOLTIMAND
In that and all things will we show our duty.

KING CLAUDIUS
We doubt it nothing: heartily farewell.

Exeunt VOLTIMAND and CORNELIUS

And now, Laertes, what's the news with you?
You told us of some suit; what is't, Laertes?
You cannot speak of reason to the Dane,
And loose your voice: what wouldst thou beg, Laertes,
That shall not be my offer, not thy asking?
The head is not more native to the heart,
The hand more instrumental to the mouth,
Than is the throne of Denmark to thy father.
What wouldst thou have, Laertes?

LAERTES
My dread lord,
Your leave and favour to return to France;
From whence though willingly I came to Denmark,
To show my duty in your coronation,

Yet now, I must confess, that duty done,
My thoughts and wishes bend again toward France
And bow them to your gracious leave and pardon.
KING CLAUDIUS
Have you your father's leave? What says Polonius?
LORD POLONIUS
He hath, my lord, wrung from me my slow leave
By laboursome petition, and at last
Upon his will I seal'd my hard consent:
I do beseech you, give him leave to go.
KING CLAUDIUS
Take thy fair hour, Laertes; time be thine,
And thy best graces spend it at thy will!
But now, my cousin Hamlet, and my son,--
HAMLET
[Aside] A little more than kin, and less than kind.
KING CLAUDIUS
How is it that the clouds still hang on you?
HAMLET
Not so, my lord; I am too much i' the sun.
QUEEN GERTRUDE
Good Hamlet, cast thy nighted colour off,
And let thine eye look like a friend on Denmark.
Do not for ever with thy vailed lids
Seek for thy noble father in the dust:
Thou know'st 'tis common; all that lives must die,
Passing through nature to eternity.
HAMLET
Ay, madam, it is common.
QUEEN GERTRUDE
If it be,
Why seems it so particular with thee?
HAMLET
Seems, madam! nay it is; I know not 'seems.'

'Tis not alone my inky cloak, good mother,
Nor customary suits of solemn black,
Nor windy suspiration of forced breath,
No, nor the fruitful river in the eye,
Nor the dejected 'havior of the visage,
Together with all forms, moods, shapes of grief,
That can denote me truly: these indeed seem,
For they are actions that a man might play:
But I have that within which passeth show;
These but the trappings and the suits of woe.

KING CLAUDIUS

'Tis sweet and commendable in your nature, Hamlet,
To give these mourning duties to your father:
But, you must know, your father lost a father;
That father lost, lost his, and the survivor bound
In filial obligation for some term
To do obsequious sorrow: but to persever
In obstinate condolement is a course
Of impious stubbornness; 'tis unmanly grief;
It shows a will most incorrect to heaven,
A heart unfortified, a mind impatient,
An understanding simple and unschool'd:
For what we know must be and is as common
As any the most vulgar thing to sense,
Why should we in our peevish opposition
Take it to heart? Fie! 'tis a fault to heaven,
A fault against the dead, a fault to nature,
To reason most absurd: whose common theme
Is death of fathers, and who still hath cried,
From the first corse till he that died to-day,
'This must be so.' We pray you, throw to earth
This unprevailing woe, and think of us
As of a father: for let the world take note,
You are the most immediate to our throne;

And with no less nobility of love
Than that which dearest father bears his son,
Do I impart toward you. For your intent
In going back to school in Wittenberg,
It is most retrograde to our desire:
And we beseech you, bend you to remain
Here, in the cheer and comfort of our eye,
Our chiefest courtier, cousin, and our son.

QUEEN GERTRUDE

Let not thy mother lose her prayers, Hamlet:
I pray thee, stay with us; go not to Wittenberg.

HAMLET

I shall in all my best obey you, madam.

KING CLAUDIUS

Why, 'tis a loving and a fair reply:
Be as ourself in Denmark. Madam, come;
This gentle and unforced accord of Hamlet
Sits smiling to my heart: in grace whereof,
No jocund health that Denmark drinks to-day,
But the great cannon to the clouds shall tell,
And the king's rouse the heavens all bruit again,
Re-speaking earthly thunder. Come away.

Exeunt all but HAMLET

HAMLET

O, that this too too solid flesh would melt
Thaw and resolve itself into a dew!
Or that the Everlasting had not fix'd
His canon 'gainst self-slaughter! O God! God!
How weary, stale, flat and unprofitable,
Seem to me all the uses of this world!
Fie on't! ah fie! 'tis an unweeded garden,
That grows to seed; things rank and gross in nature
Possess it merely. That it should come to this!

But two months dead: nay, not so much, not two:
So excellent a king; that was, to this,
Hyperion to a satyr; so loving to my mother
That he might not beteem the winds of heaven
Visit her face too roughly. Heaven and earth!
Must I remember? why, she would hang on him,
As if increase of appetite had grown
By what it fed on: and yet, within a month--
Let me not think on't--Frailty, thy name is woman!--
A little month, or ere those shoes were old
With which she follow'd my poor father's body,
Like Niobe, all tears:--why she, even she--
O, God! a beast, that wants discourse of reason,
Would have mourn'd longer--married with my uncle,
My father's brother, but no more like my father
Than I to Hercules: within a month:
Ere yet the salt of most unrighteous tears
Had left the flushing in her galled eyes,
She married. O, most wicked speed, to post
With such dexterity to incestuous sheets!
It is not nor it cannot come to good:
But break, my heart; for I must hold my tongue.

Enter HORATIO, MARCELLUS, and BERNARDO

HORATIO
　Hail to your lordship!
HAMLET
　I am glad to see you well:
　Horatio,--or I do forget myself.
HORATIO
　The same, my lord, and your poor servant ever.
HAMLET
　Sir, my good friend; I'll change that name with you:

And what make you from Wittenberg, Horatio?
Marcellus?
MARCELLUS

My good lord--
HAMLET

I am very glad to see you. Good even, sir.
But what, in faith, make you from Wittenberg?
HORATIO

A truant disposition, good my lord.
HAMLET

I would not hear your enemy say so,
Nor shall you do mine ear that violence,
To make it truster of your own report
Against yourself: I know you are no truant.
But what is your affair in Elsinore?
We'll teach you to drink deep ere you depart.
HORATIO

My lord, I came to see your father's funeral.
HAMLET

I pray thee, do not mock me, fellow-student;
I think it was to see my mother's wedding.
HORATIO

Indeed, my lord, it follow'd hard upon.
HAMLET

Thrift, thrift, Horatio! the funeral baked meats
Did coldly furnish forth the marriage tables.
Would I had met my dearest foe in heaven
Or ever I had seen that day, Horatio!
My father!--methinks I see my father.
HORATIO

Where, my lord?
HAMLET

In my mind's eye, Horatio.
HORATIO

I saw him once; he was a goodly king.

HAMLET

He was a man, take him for all in all,
I shall not look upon his like again.

HORATIO

My lord, I think I saw him yesternight.

HAMLET

Saw? who?

HORATIO

My lord, the king your father.

HAMLET

The king my father!

HORATIO

Season your admiration for awhile
With an attent ear, till I may deliver,
Upon the witness of these gentlemen,
This marvel to you.

HAMLET

For God's love, let me hear.

HORATIO

Two nights together had these gentlemen,
Marcellus and Bernardo, on their watch,
In the dead vast and middle of the night,
Been thus encounter'd. A figure like your father,
Armed at point exactly, cap-a-pe,
Appears before them, and with solemn march
Goes slow and stately by them: thrice he walk'd
By their oppress'd and fear-surprised eyes,
Within his truncheon's length; whilst they, distilled
Almost to jelly with the act of fear,
Stand dumb and speak not to him. This to me
In dreadful secrecy impart they did;
And I with them the third night kept the watch;
Where, as they had deliver'd, both in time,

Form of the thing, each word made true and good,
The apparition comes: I knew your father;
These hands are not more like.

HAMLET

But where was this?

MARCELLUS

My lord, upon the platform where we watch'd.

HAMLET

Did you not speak to it?

HORATIO

My lord, I did;
But answer made it none: yet once methought
It lifted up its head and did address
Itself to motion, like as it would speak;
But even then the morning cock crew loud,
And at the sound it shrunk in haste away,
And vanish'd from our sight.

HAMLET

'Tis very strange.

HORATIO

As I do live, my honour'd lord, 'tis true;
And we did think it writ down in our duty
To let you know of it.

HAMLET

Indeed, indeed, sirs, but this troubles me.
Hold you the watch to-night?

MARCELLUS BERNARDO

We do, my lord.

HAMLET

Arm'd, say you?

MARCELLUS BERNARDO

Arm'd, my lord.

HAMLET

From top to toe?

MARCELLUS BERNARDO
  My lord, from head to foot.
HAMLET
  Then saw you not his face?
HORATIO
  O, yes, my lord; he wore his beaver up.
HAMLET
  What, look'd he frowningly?
HORATIO
  A countenance more in sorrow than in anger.
HAMLET
  Pale or red?
HORATIO
  Nay, very pale.
HAMLET
  And fix'd his eyes upon you?
HORATIO
  Most constantly.
HAMLET
  I would I had been there.
HORATIO
  It would have much amazed you.
HAMLET
  Very like, very like. Stay'd it long?
HORATIO
  While one with moderate haste might tell a hundred.
MARCELLUS BERNARDO
  Longer, longer.
HORATIO
  Not when I saw't.
HAMLET
  His beard was grizzled--no?
HORATIO
  It was, as I have seen it in his life,

A sable silver'd.

HAMLET

I will watch to-night;
Perchance 'twill walk again.

HORATIO

I warrant it will.

HAMLET

If it assume my noble father's person,
I'll speak to it, though hell itself should gape
And bid me hold my peace. I pray you all,
If you have hitherto conceal'd this sight,
Let it be tenable in your silence still;
And whatsoever else shall hap to-night,
Give it an understanding, but no tongue:
I will requite your loves. So, fare you well:
Upon the platform, 'twixt eleven and twelve,
I'll visit you.

All

Our duty to your honour.

HAMLET

Your loves, as mine to you: farewell.

Exeunt all but HAMLET

My father's spirit in arms! all is not well;
I doubt some foul play: would the night were come!
Till then sit still, my soul: foul deeds will rise,
Though all the earth o'erwhelm them, to men's eyes.

Exit

SCENE III.

A room in Polonius' house.

Enter LAERTES and OPHELIA

LAERTES

My necessaries are embark'd: farewell:
And, sister, as the winds give benefit
And convoy is assistant, do not sleep,
But let me hear from you.

OPHELIA

Do you doubt that?

LAERTES

For Hamlet and the trifling of his favour,
Hold it a fashion and a toy in blood,
A violet in the youth of primy nature,
Forward, not permanent, sweet, not lasting,
The perfume and suppliance of a minute; No more.

OPHELIA

No more but so?

LAERTES

Think it no more;
For nature, crescent, does not grow alone
In thews and bulk, but, as this temple waxes,
The inward service of the mind and soul
Grows wide withal. Perhaps he loves you now,
And now no soil nor cautel doth besmirch
The virtue of his will: but you must fear,
His greatness weigh'd, his will is not his own;
For he himself is subject to his birth:
He may not, as unvalued persons do,
Carve for himself; for on his choice depends
The safety and health of this whole state;
And therefore must his choice be circumscribed
Unto the voice and yielding of that body

Whereof he is the head. Then if he says he loves you,
It fits your wisdom so far to believe it
As he in his particular act and place
May give his saying deed; which is no further
Than the main voice of Denmark goes withal.
Then weigh what loss your honour may sustain,
If with too credent ear you list his songs,
Or lose your heart, or your chaste treasure open
To his unmaster'd importunity.
Fear it, Ophelia, fear it, my dear sister,
And keep you in the rear of your affection,
Out of the shot and danger of desire.
The chariest maid is prodigal enough,
If she unmask her beauty to the moon:
Virtue itself 'scapes not calumnious strokes:
The canker galls the infants of the spring,
Too oft before their buttons be disclosed,
And in the morn and liquid dew of youth
Contagious blastments are most imminent.
Be wary then; best safety lies in fear:
Youth to itself rebels, though none else near.
OPHELIA
I shall the effect of this good lesson keep,
As watchman to my heart. But, good my brother,
Do not, as some ungracious pastors do,
Show me the steep and thorny way to heaven;
Whiles, like a puff'd and reckless libertine,
Himself the primrose path of dalliance treads,
And recks not his own rede.
LAERTES
O, fear me not.
I stay too long: but here my father comes.

Enter POLONIUS

A double blessing is a double grace,
Occasion smiles upon a second leave.

LORD POLONIUS

Yet here, Laertes! aboard, aboard, for shame!
The wind sits in the shoulder of your sail,
And you are stay'd for. There; my blessing with thee!
And these few precepts in thy memory
See thou character. Give thy thoughts no tongue,
Nor any unproportioned thought his act.
Be thou familiar, but by no means vulgar.
Those friends thou hast, and their adoption tried,
Grapple them to thy soul with hoops of steel;
But do not dull thy palm with entertainment
Of each new-hatch'd, unfledged comrade. Beware
Of entrance to a quarrel, but being in,
Bear't that the opposed may beware of thee.
Give every man thy ear, but few thy voice;
Take each man's censure, but reserve thy judgment.
Costly thy habit as thy purse can buy,
But not express'd in fancy; rich, not gaudy;
For the apparel oft proclaims the man,
And they in France of the best rank and station
Are of a most select and generous chief in that.
Neither a borrower nor a lender be;
For loan oft loses both itself and friend,
And borrowing dulls the edge of husbandry.
This above all: to thine ownself be true,
And it must follow, as the night the day,
Thou canst not then be false to any man.
Farewell: my blessing season this in thee!

LAERTES

Most humbly do I take my leave, my lord.

LORD POLONIUS

The time invites you; go; your servants tend.

LAERTES
Farewell, Ophelia; and remember well
What I have said to you.
OPHELIA
'Tis in my memory lock'd,
And you yourself shall keep the key of it.
LAERTES
Farewell.

Exit

LORD POLONIUS
What is't, Ophelia, be hath said to you?
OPHELIA
So please you, something touching the Lord Hamlet.
LORD POLONIUS
Marry, well bethought:
'Tis told me, he hath very oft of late
Given private time to you; and you yourself
Have of your audience been most free and bounteous:
If it be so, as so 'tis put on me,
And that in way of caution, I must tell you,
You do not understand yourself so clearly
As it behoves my daughter and your honour.
What is between you? give me up the truth.
OPHELIA
He hath, my lord, of late made many tenders
Of his affection to me.
LORD POLONIUS
Affection! pooh! you speak like a green girl,
Unsifted in such perilous circumstance.
Do you believe his tenders, as you call them?
OPHELIA
I do not know, my lord, what I should think.
LORD POLONIUS

Marry, I'll teach you: think yourself a baby;
That you have ta'en these tenders for true pay,
Which are not sterling. Tender yourself more dearly;
Or--not to crack the wind of the poor phrase,
Running it thus--you'll tender me a fool.

OPHELIA

My lord, he hath importuned me with love
In honourable fashion.

LORD POLONIUS

Ay, fashion you may call it; go to, go to.

OPHELIA

And hath given countenance to his speech, my lord,
With almost all the holy vows of heaven.

LORD POLONIUS

Ay, springes to catch woodcocks. I do know,
When the blood burns, how prodigal the soul
Lends the tongue vows: these blazes, daughter,
Giving more light than heat, extinct in both,
Even in their promise, as it is a-making,
You must not take for fire. From this time
Be somewhat scanter of your maiden presence;
Set your entreatments at a higher rate
Than a command to parley. For Lord Hamlet,
Believe so much in him, that he is young
And with a larger tether may he walk
Than may be given you: in few, Ophelia,
Do not believe his vows; for they are brokers,
Not of that dye which their investments show,
But mere implorators of unholy suits,
Breathing like sanctified and pious bawds,
The better to beguile. This is for all:
I would not, in plain terms, from this time forth,
Have you so slander any moment leisure,
As to give words or talk with the Lord Hamlet.

Look to't, I charge you: come your ways.
OPHELIA
I shall obey, my lord.

Exeunt

SCENE IV.

The platform.

Enter HAMLET, HORATIO, and MARCELLUS

HAMLET

The air bites shrewdly; it is very cold.
HORATIO
It is a nipping and an eager air.
HAMLET
What hour now?
HORATIO
I think it lacks of twelve.
HAMLET
No, it is struck.
HORATIO
Indeed? I heard it not: then it draws near the season
Wherein the spirit held his wont to walk.

A flourish of trumpets, and ordnance shot off, within

What does this mean, my lord?
HAMLET
The king doth wake to-night and takes his rouse,
Keeps wassail, and the swaggering up-spring reels;
And, as he drains his draughts of Rhenish down,
The kettle-drum and trumpet thus bray out
The triumph of his pledge.
HORATIO
Is it a custom?

HAMLET

    Ay, marry, is't:
    But to my mind, though I am native here
    And to the manner born, it is a custom
    More honour'd in the breach than the observance.
    This heavy-headed revel east and west
    Makes us traduced and tax'd of other nations:
    They clepe us drunkards, and with swinish phrase
    Soil our addition; and indeed it takes
    From our achievements, though perform'd at height,
    The pith and marrow of our attribute.
    So, oft it chances in particular men,
    That for some vicious mole of nature in them,
    As, in their birth--wherein they are not guilty,
    Since nature cannot choose his origin--
    By the o'ergrowth of some complexion,
    Oft breaking down the pales and forts of reason,
    Or by some habit that too much o'er-leavens
    The form of plausive manners, that these men,
    Carrying, I say, the stamp of one defect,
    Being nature's livery, or fortune's star,--
    Their virtues else--be they as pure as grace,
    As infinite as man may undergo--
    Shall in the general censure take corruption
    From that particular fault: the dram of eale
    Doth all the noble substance of a doubt
    To his own scandal.

HORATIO

    Look, my lord, it comes!

Enter Ghost

HAMLET

    Angels and ministers of grace defend us!
    Be thou a spirit of health or goblin damn'd,

Bring with thee airs from heaven or blasts from hell,
Be thy intents wicked or charitable,
Thou comest in such a questionable shape
That I will speak to thee: I'll call thee Hamlet,
King, father, royal Dane: O, answer me!
Let me not burst in ignorance; but tell
Why thy canonized bones, hearsed in death,
Have burst their cerements; why the sepulchre,
Wherein we saw thee quietly inurn'd,
Hath oped his ponderous and marble jaws,
To cast thee up again. What may this mean,
That thou, dead corse, again in complete steel
Revisit'st thus the glimpses of the moon,
Making night hideous; and we fools of nature
So horridly to shake our disposition
With thoughts beyond the reaches of our souls?
Say, why is this? wherefore? what should we do?

Ghost beckons HAMLET

HORATIO
    It beckons you to go away with it,
    As if it some impartment did desire
    To you alone.
MARCELLUS
    Look, with what courteous action
    It waves you to a more removed ground:
    But do not go with it.
HORATIO
    No, by no means.
HAMLET
    It will not speak; then I will follow it.
HORATIO
    Do not, my lord.
HAMLET

Why, what should be the fear?
I do not set my life in a pin's fee;
And for my soul, what can it do to that,
Being a thing immortal as itself?
It waves me forth again: I'll follow it.

HORATIO

What if it tempt you toward the flood, my lord,
Or to the dreadful summit of the cliff
That beetles o'er his base into the sea,
And there assume some other horrible form,
Which might deprive your sovereignty of reason
And draw you into madness? think of it:
The very place puts toys of desperation,
Without more motive, into every brain
That looks so many fathoms to the sea
And hears it roar beneath.

HAMLET

It waves me still.
Go on; I'll follow thee.

MARCELLUS

You shall not go, my lord.

HAMLET

Hold off your hands.

HORATIO

Be ruled; you shall not go.

HAMLET

My fate cries out,
And makes each petty artery in this body
As hardy as the Nemean lion's nerve.
Still am I call'd. Unhand me, gentlemen.
By heaven, I'll make a ghost of him that lets me!
I say, away! Go on; I'll follow thee.

Exeunt Ghost and HAMLET

HORATIO
He waxes desperate with imagination.
MARCELLUS
Let's follow; 'tis not fit thus to obey him.
HORATIO
Have after. To what issue will this come?
MARCELLUS
Something is rotten in the state of Denmark.
HORATIO
Heaven will direct it.
MARCELLUS
Nay, let's follow him.

Exeunt

SCENE V.

Another part of the platform.

Enter GHOST and HAMLET

HAMLET
Where wilt thou lead me? speak; I'll go no further.
Ghost
Mark me.
HAMLET
I will.
Ghost
My hour is almost come,
When I to sulphurous and tormenting flames
Must render up myself.
HAMLET
Alas, poor ghost!
Ghost
Pity me not, but lend thy serious hearing
To what I shall unfold.

HAMLET

Speak; I am bound to hear.

Ghost

So art thou to revenge, when thou shalt hear.

HAMLET

What?

Ghost

I am thy father's spirit,
Doom'd for a certain term to walk the night,
And for the day confined to fast in fires,
Till the foul crimes done in my days of nature
Are burnt and purged away. But that I am forbid
To tell the secrets of my prison-house,
I could a tale unfold whose lightest word
Would harrow up thy soul, freeze thy young blood,
Make thy two eyes, like stars, start from their spheres,
Thy knotted and combined locks to part
And each particular hair to stand on end,
Like quills upon the fretful porpentine:
But this eternal blazon must not be
To ears of flesh and blood. List, list, O, list!
If thou didst ever thy dear father love--

HAMLET

O God!

Ghost

Revenge his foul and most unnatural murder.

HAMLET

Murder!

Ghost

Murder most foul, as in the best it is;
But this most foul, strange and unnatural.

HAMLET

Haste me to know't, that I, with wings as swift
As meditation or the thoughts of love,

May sweep to my revenge.
Ghost
    I find thee apt;
    And duller shouldst thou be than the fat weed
    That roots itself in ease on Lethe wharf,
    Wouldst thou not stir in this. Now, Hamlet, hear:
    'Tis given out that, sleeping in my orchard,
    A serpent stung me; so the whole ear of Denmark
    Is by a forged process of my death
    Rankly abused: but know, thou noble youth,
    The serpent that did sting thy father's life
    Now wears his crown.
HAMLET
    O my prophetic soul! My uncle!
Ghost
    Ay, that incestuous, that adulterate beast,
    With witchcraft of his wit, with traitorous gifts,
    O wicked wit and gifts, that have the power
    So to seduce!--won to his shameful lust
    The will of my most seeming-virtuous queen:
    O Hamlet, what a falling-off was there!
    From me, whose love was of that dignity
    That it went hand in hand even with the vow
    I made to her in marriage, and to decline
    Upon a wretch whose natural gifts were poor
    To those of mine!
    But virtue, as it never will be moved,
    Though lewdness court it in a shape of heaven,
    So lust, though to a radiant angel link'd,
    Will sate itself in a celestial bed,
    And prey on garbage.
    But, soft! methinks I scent the morning air;
    Brief let me be. Sleeping within my orchard,
    My custom always of the afternoon,

Upon my secure hour thy uncle stole,
With juice of cursed hebenon in a vial,
And in the porches of my ears did pour
The leperous distilment; whose effect
Holds such an enmity with blood of man
That swift as quicksilver it courses through
The natural gates and alleys of the body,
And with a sudden vigour doth posset
And curd, like eager droppings into milk,
The thin and wholesome blood: so did it mine;
And a most instant tetter bark'd about,
Most lazar-like, with vile and loathsome crust,
All my smooth body.
Thus was I, sleeping, by a brother's hand
Of life, of crown, of queen, at once dispatch'd:
Cut off even in the blossoms of my sin,
Unhousel'd, disappointed, unanel'd,
No reckoning made, but sent to my account
With all my imperfections on my head:
O, horrible! O, horrible! most horrible!
If thou hast nature in thee, bear it not;
Let not the royal bed of Denmark be
A couch for luxury and damned incest.
But, howsoever thou pursuest this act,
Taint not thy mind, nor let thy soul contrive
Against thy mother aught: leave her to heaven
And to those thorns that in her bosom lodge,
To prick and sting her. Fare thee well at once!
The glow-worm shows the matin to be near,
And 'gins to pale his uneffectual fire:
Adieu, adieu! Hamlet, remember me.

Exit

HAMLET

O all you host of heaven! O earth! what else?
And shall I couple hell? O, fie! Hold, hold, my heart;
And you, my sinews, grow not instant old,
But bear me stiffly up. Remember thee!
Ay, thou poor ghost, while memory holds a seat
In this distracted globe. Remember thee!
Yea, from the table of my memory
I'll wipe away all trivial fond records,
All saws of books, all forms, all pressures past,
That youth and observation copied there;
And thy commandment all alone shall live
Within the book and volume of my brain,
Unmix'd with baser matter: yes, by heaven!
O most pernicious woman!
O villain, villain, smiling, damned villain!
My tables,--meet it is I set it down,
That one may smile, and smile, and be a villain;
At least I'm sure it may be so in Denmark:

Writing

So, uncle, there you are. Now to my word;
It is 'Adieu, adieu! remember me.'
I have sworn 't.
MARCELLUS HORATIO
  [Within] My lord, my lord,--
MARCELLUS
  [Within]   Lord Hamlet,--
HORATIO
  [Within]   Heaven secure him!
HAMLET
  So be it!
HORATIO
  [Within] Hillo, ho, ho, my lord!
HAMLET

Hillo, ho, ho, boy! come, bird, come.

Enter HORATIO and MARCELLUS

MARCELLUS
   How is't, my noble lord?
HORATIO
   What news, my lord?
HAMLET
   O, wonderful!
HORATIO
   Good my lord, tell it.
HAMLET
   No; you'll reveal it.
HORATIO
   Not I, my lord, by heaven.
MARCELLUS
   Nor I, my lord.
HAMLET
   How say you, then; would heart of man once think it?
   But you'll be secret?
HORATIO MARCELLUS
   Ay, by heaven, my lord.
HAMLET
   There's ne'er a villain dwelling in all Denmark
   But he's an arrant knave.
HORATIO
   There needs no ghost, my lord, come from the grave
   To tell us this.
HAMLET
   Why, right; you are i' the right;
   And so, without more circumstance at all,
   I hold it fit that we shake hands and part:
   You, as your business and desire shall point you;
   For every man has business and desire,

Such as it is; and for mine own poor part,
Look you, I'll go pray.
HORATIO
These are but wild and whirling words, my lord.
HAMLET
I'm sorry they offend you, heartily;
Yes, 'faith heartily.
HORATIO
There's no offence, my lord.
HAMLET
Yes, by Saint Patrick, but there is, Horatio,
And much offence too. Touching this vision here,
It is an honest ghost, that let me tell you:
For your desire to know what is between us,
O'ermaster 't as you may. And now, good friends,
As you are friends, scholars and soldiers,
Give me one poor request.
HORATIO
What is't, my lord? we will.
HAMLET
Never make known what you have seen to-night.
HORATIO MARCELLUS
My lord, we will not.
HAMLET
Nay, but swear't.
HORATIO
In faith,
My lord, not I.
MARCELLUS
Nor I, my lord, in faith.
HAMLET
Upon my sword.
MARCELLUS
We have sworn, my lord, already.

HAMLET

Indeed, upon my sword, indeed.

Ghost

[Beneath] Swear.

HAMLET

Ah, ha, boy! say'st thou so? art thou there,
truepenny?

Come on--you hear this fellow in the cellarage--

Consent to swear.

HORATIO

Propose the oath, my lord.

HAMLET

Never to speak of this that you have seen,

Swear by my sword.

Ghost

[Beneath] Swear.

HAMLET

Hic et ubique? then we'll shift our ground.

Come hither, gentlemen,

And lay your hands again upon my sword:

Never to speak of this that you have heard,

Swear by my sword.

Ghost

[Beneath] Swear.

HAMLET

Well said, old mole! canst work i' the earth so fast?

A worthy pioner! Once more remove, good friends.

HORATIO

O day and night, but this is wondrous strange!

HAMLET

And therefore as a stranger give it welcome.

There are more things in heaven and earth, Horatio,

Than are dreamt of in your philosophy. But come;

Here, as before, never, so help you mercy,

How strange or odd soe'er I bear myself,
As I perchance hereafter shall think meet
To put an antic disposition on,
That you, at such times seeing me, never shall,
With arms encumber'd thus, or this headshake,
Or by pronouncing of some doubtful phrase,
As 'Well, well, we know,' or 'We could, an if we would,'
Or 'If we list to speak,' or 'There be, an if they might,'
Or such ambiguous giving out, to note
That you know aught of me: this not to do,
So grace and mercy at your most need help you, Swear.
Ghost
    [Beneath] Swear.
HAMLET
    Rest, rest, perturbed spirit!

They swear

So, gentlemen,
With all my love I do commend me to you:
And what so poor a man as Hamlet is
May do, to express his love and friending to you,
God willing, shall not lack. Let us go in together;
And still your fingers on your lips, I pray.
The time is out of joint: O cursed spite,
That ever I was born to set it right!
Nay, come, let's go together.

Exeunt

ACT II

SCENE I.

A room in POLONIUS' house.

Enter POLONIUS and REYNALDO

LORD POLONIUS
Give him this money and these notes, Reynaldo.
REYNALDO
I will, my lord.
LORD POLONIUS
You shall do marvellous wisely, good Reynaldo,
Before you visit him, to make inquire
Of his behavior.
REYNALDO
My lord, I did intend it.
LORD POLONIUS
Marry, well said; very well said. Look you, sir,
Inquire me first what Danskers are in Paris;
And how, and who, what means, and where they keep,
What company, at what expense; and finding
By this encompassment and drift of question
That they do know my son, come you more nearer
Than your particular demands will touch it:
Take you, as 'twere, some distant knowledge of him;
As thus, 'I know his father and his friends,
And in part him: ' do you mark this, Reynaldo?
REYNALDO
Ay, very well, my lord.
LORD POLONIUS
'And in part him; but' you may say 'not well:
But, if't be he I mean, he's very wild;
Addicted so and so:' and there put on him

43

What forgeries you please; marry, none so rank
As may dishonour him; take heed of that;
But, sir, such wanton, wild and usual slips
As are companions noted and most known
To youth and liberty.
REYNALDO
　　As gaming, my lord.
LORD POLONIUS
　　Ay, or drinking, fencing, swearing, quarrelling,
　　Drabbing: you may go so far.
REYNALDO
　　My lord, that would dishonour him.
LORD POLONIUS
　　'Faith, no; as you may season it in the charge
　　You must not put another scandal on him,
　　That he is open to incontinency;
　　That's not my meaning: but breathe his faults so quaintly
　　That they may seem the taints of liberty,
　　The flash and outbreak of a fiery mind,
　　A savageness in unreclaimed blood,
　　Of general assault.
REYNALDO
　　But, my good lord,--
LORD POLONIUS
　　Wherefore should you do this?
REYNALDO
　　Ay, my lord,
　　I would know that.
LORD POLONIUS
　　Marry, sir, here's my drift;
　　And I believe, it is a fetch of wit:
　　You laying these slight sullies on my son,
　　As 'twere a thing a little soil'd i' the working, Mark you,
　　Your party in converse, him you would sound,

Having ever seen in the prenominate crimes
The youth you breathe of guilty, be assured
He closes with you in this consequence;
'Good sir,' or so, or 'friend,' or 'gentleman,'
According to the phrase or the addition
Of man and country.

REYNALDO

Very good, my lord.

LORD POLONIUS

And then, sir, does he this--he does--what was I
about to say? By the mass, I was about to say
something: where did I leave?

REYNALDO

At 'closes in the consequence,' at 'friend or so,'
and 'gentleman.'

LORD POLONIUS

At 'closes in the consequence,' ay, marry;
He closes thus: 'I know the gentleman;
I saw him yesterday, or t' other day,
Or then, or then; with such, or such; and, as you say,
There was a' gaming; there o'ertook in's rouse;
There falling out at tennis:' or perchance,
'I saw him enter such a house of sale,'
Videlicet, a brothel, or so forth.
See you now;
Your bait of falsehood takes this carp of truth:
And thus do we of wisdom and of reach,
With windlasses and with assays of bias,
By indirections find directions out:
So by my former lecture and advice,
Shall you my son. You have me, have you not?

REYNALDO

My lord, I have.

LORD POLONIUS

God be wi' you; fare you well.
REYNALDO
Good my lord!
LORD POLONIUS
Observe his inclination in yourself.
REYNALDO
I shall, my lord.
LORD POLONIUS
And let him ply his music.
REYNALDO
Well, my lord.
LORD POLONIUS
Farewell!

Exit REYNALDO

Enter OPHELIA

How now, Ophelia! what's the matter?
OPHELIA
O, my lord, my lord, I have been so affrighted!
LORD POLONIUS
With what, i' the name of God?
OPHELIA
My lord, as I was sewing in my closet,
Lord Hamlet, with his doublet all unbraced;
No hat upon his head; his stockings foul'd,
Ungarter'd, and down-gyved to his ancle;
Pale as his shirt; his knees knocking each other;
And with a look so piteous in purport
As if he had been loosed out of hell
To speak of horrors,--he comes before me.
LORD POLONIUS
Mad for thy love?

OPHELIA

My lord, I do not know;
But truly, I do fear it.

LORD POLONIUS

What said he?

OPHELIA

He took me by the wrist and held me hard;
Then goes he to the length of all his arm;
And, with his other hand thus o'er his brow,
He falls to such perusal of my face
As he would draw it. Long stay'd he so;
At last, a little shaking of mine arm
And thrice his head thus waving up and down,
He raised a sigh so piteous and profound
As it did seem to shatter all his bulk
And end his being: that done, he lets me go:
And, with his head over his shoulder turn'd,
He seem'd to find his way without his eyes;
For out o' doors he went without their helps,
And, to the last, bended their light on me.

LORD POLONIUS

Come, go with me: I will go seek the king.
This is the very ecstasy of love,
Whose violent property fordoes itself
And leads the will to desperate undertakings
As oft as any passion under heaven
That does afflict our natures. I am sorry.
What, have you given him any hard words of late?

OPHELIA

No, my good lord, but, as you did command,
I did repel his fetters and denied
His access to me.

LORD POLONIUS

That hath made him mad.

I am sorry that with better heed and judgment
I had not quoted him: I fear'd he did but trifle,
And meant to wreck thee; but, beshrew my jealousy!
By heaven, it is as proper to our age
To cast beyond ourselves in our opinions
As it is common for the younger sort
To lack discretion. Come, go we to the king:
This must be known; which, being kept close, might move
More grief to hide than hate to utter love.

Exeunt

SCENE II.

A room in the castle.

*Enter KING CLAUDIUS, QUEEN GERTRUDE,
ROSENCRANTZ, GUILDENSTERN, and Attendants*

KING CLAUDIUS
Welcome, dear Rosencrantz and Guildenstern!
Moreover that we much did long to see you,
The need we have to use you did provoke
Our hasty sending. Something have you heard
Of Hamlet's transformation; so call it,
Sith nor the exterior nor the inward man
Resembles that it was. What it should be,
More than his father's death, that thus hath put him
So much from the understanding of himself,
I cannot dream of: I entreat you both,
That, being of so young days brought up with him,
And sith so neighbour'd to his youth and havior,
That you vouchsafe your rest here in our court
Some little time: so by your companies
To draw him on to pleasures, and to gather,

So much as from occasion you may glean,
Whether aught, to us unknown, afflicts him thus,
That, open'd, lies within our remedy.
QUEEN GERTRUDE
Good gentlemen, he hath much talk'd of you;
And sure I am two men there are not living
To whom he more adheres. If it will please you
To show us so much gentry and good will
As to expend your time with us awhile,
For the supply and profit of our hope,
Your visitation shall receive such thanks
As fits a king's remembrance.
ROSENCRANTZ
Both your majesties
Might, by the sovereign power you have of us,
Put your dread pleasures more into command
Than to entreaty.
GUILDENSTERN
But we both obey,
And here give up ourselves, in the full bent
To lay our service freely at your feet,
To be commanded.
KING CLAUDIUS
Thanks, Rosencrantz and gentle Guildenstern.
QUEEN GERTRUDE
Thanks, Guildenstern and gentle Rosencrantz:
And I beseech you instantly to visit
My too much changed son. Go, some of you,
And bring these gentlemen where Hamlet is.
GUILDENSTERN
Heavens make our presence and our practises
Pleasant and helpful to him!
QUEEN GERTRUDE
Ay, amen!

Exeunt ROSENCRANTZ, GUILDENSTERN, and some Attendants

Enter POLONIUS

LORD POLONIUS
    The ambassadors from Norway, my good lord,
    Are joyfully return'd.
KING CLAUDIUS
    Thou still hast been the father of good news.
LORD POLONIUS
    Have I, my lord? I assure my good liege,
    I hold my duty, as I hold my soul,
    Both to my God and to my gracious king:
    And I do think, or else this brain of mine
    Hunts not the trail of policy so sure
    As it hath used to do, that I have found
    The very cause of Hamlet's lunacy.
KING CLAUDIUS
    O, speak of that; that do I long to hear.
LORD POLONIUS
    Give first admittance to the ambassadors;
    My news shall be the fruit to that great feast.
KING CLAUDIUS
    Thyself do grace to them, and bring them in.

Exit POLONIUS

    He tells me, my dear Gertrude, he hath found
    The head and source of all your son's distemper.
QUEEN GERTRUDE
    I doubt it is no other but the main;
    His father's death, and our o'erhasty marriage.
KING CLAUDIUS
    Well, we shall sift him.

Re-enter POLONIUS, with VOLTIMAND and CORNELIUS

Welcome, my good friends!
Say, Voltimand, what from our brother Norway?
VOLTIMAND
    Most fair return of greetings and desires.
    Upon our first, he sent out to suppress
    His nephew's levies; which to him appear'd
    To be a preparation 'gainst the Polack;
    But, better look'd into, he truly found
    It was against your highness: whereat grieved,
    That so his sickness, age and impotence
    Was falsely borne in hand, sends out arrests
    On Fortinbras; which he, in brief, obeys;
    Receives rebuke from Norway, and in fine
    Makes vow before his uncle never more
    To give the assay of arms against your majesty.
    Whereon old Norway, overcome with joy,
    Gives him three thousand crowns in annual fee,
    And his commission to employ those soldiers,
    So levied as before, against the Polack:
    With an entreaty, herein further shown,

Giving a paper

    That it might please you to give quiet pass
    Through your dominions for this enterprise,
    On such regards of safety and allowance
    As therein are set down.
KING CLAUDIUS
    It likes us well;
    And at our more consider'd time well read,
    Answer, and think upon this business.
    Meantime we thank you for your well-took labour:
    Go to your rest; at night we'll feast together:

Most welcome home!

Exeunt VOLTIMAND and CORNELIUS

LORD POLONIUS
This business is well ended.
My liege, and madam, to expostulate
What majesty should be, what duty is,
Why day is day, night night, and time is time,
Were nothing but to waste night, day and time.
Therefore, since brevity is the soul of wit,
And tediousness the limbs and outward flourishes,
I will be brief: your noble son is mad:
Mad call I it; for, to define true madness,
What is't but to be nothing else but mad?
But let that go.
QUEEN GERTRUDE
More matter, with less art.
LORD POLONIUS
Madam, I swear I use no art at all.
That he is mad, 'tis true: 'tis true 'tis pity;
And pity 'tis 'tis true: a foolish figure;
But farewell it, for I will use no art.
Mad let us grant him, then: and now remains
That we find out the cause of this effect,
Or rather say, the cause of this defect,
For this effect defective comes by cause:
Thus it remains, and the remainder thus. Perpend.
I have a daughter--have while she is mine--
Who, in her duty and obedience, mark,
Hath given me this: now gather, and surmise.

Reads

'To the celestial and my soul's idol, the most

beautified Ophelia,'--
That's an ill phrase, a vile phrase; 'beautified' is
a vile phrase: but you shall hear. Thus:

Reads

'In her excellent white bosom, these, & c.'
QUEEN GERTRUDE
Came this from Hamlet to her?
LORD POLONIUS
Good madam, stay awhile; I will be faithful.

Reads

'Doubt thou the stars are fire;
Doubt that the sun doth move;
Doubt truth to be a liar;
But never doubt I love.
'O dear Ophelia, I am ill at these numbers;
I have not art to reckon my groans: but that
I love thee best, O most best, believe it. Adieu.
'Thine evermore most dear lady, whilst
this machine is to him, HAMLET.'
This, in obedience, hath my daughter shown me,
And more above, hath his solicitings,
As they fell out by time, by means and place,
All given to mine ear.
KING CLAUDIUS
But how hath she
Received his love?
LORD POLONIUS
What do you think of me?
KING CLAUDIUS
As of a man faithful and honourable.
LORD POLONIUS

I would fain prove so. But what might you think,
When I had seen this hot love on the wing--
As I perceived it, I must tell you that,
Before my daughter told me--what might you,
Or my dear majesty your queen here, think,
If I had play'd the desk or table-book,
Or given my heart a winking, mute and dumb,
Or look'd upon this love with idle sight;
What might you think? No, I went round to work,
And my young mistress thus I did bespeak:
'Lord Hamlet is a prince, out of thy star;
This must not be:' and then I precepts gave her,
That she should lock herself from his resort,
Admit no messengers, receive no tokens.
Which done, she took the fruits of my advice;
And he, repulsed--a short tale to make--
Fell into a sadness, then into a fast,
Thence to a watch, thence into a weakness,
Thence to a lightness, and, by this declension,
Into the madness wherein now he raves,
And all we mourn for.

KING CLAUDIUS
Do you think 'tis this?

QUEEN GERTRUDE
It may be, very likely.

LORD POLONIUS
Hath there been such a time--I'd fain know that-
That I have positively said 'Tis so,'
When it proved otherwise?

KING CLAUDIUS
Not that I know.

LORD POLONIUS
[Pointing to his head and shoulder]
Take this from this, if this be otherwise:

54

If circumstances lead me, I will find
Where truth is hid, though it were hid indeed
Within the centre.
KING CLAUDIUS
How may we try it further?
LORD POLONIUS
You know, sometimes he walks four hours together
Here in the lobby.
QUEEN GERTRUDE
So he does indeed.
LORD POLONIUS
At such a time I'll loose my daughter to him:
Be you and I behind an arras then;
Mark the encounter: if he love her not
And be not from his reason fall'n thereon,
Let me be no assistant for a state,
But keep a farm and carters.
KING CLAUDIUS
We will try it.
QUEEN GERTRUDE
But, look, where sadly the poor wretch comes reading.
LORD POLONIUS
Away, I do beseech you, both away:
I'll board him presently.

*Exeunt KING CLAUDIUS, QUEEN GERTRUDE, and
Attendants*

Enter HAMLET, reading

O, give me leave:
How does my good Lord Hamlet?
HAMLET
Well, God-a-mercy.

LORD POLONIUS

Do you know me, my lord?

HAMLET

Excellent well; you are a fishmonger.

LORD POLONIUS

Not I, my lord.

HAMLET

Then I would you were so honest a man.

LORD POLONIUS

Honest, my lord!

HAMLET

Ay, sir; to be honest, as this world goes, is to be
one man picked out of ten thousand.

LORD POLONIUS

That's very true, my lord.

HAMLET

For if the sun breed maggots in a dead dog, being a
god kissing carrion,--Have you a daughter?

LORD POLONIUS

I have, my lord.

HAMLET

Let her not walk i' the sun: conception is a
blessing: but not as your daughter may conceive.
Friend, look to 't.

LORD POLONIUS

[Aside] How say you by that? Still harping on my
daughter: yet he knew me not at first; he said I
was a fishmonger: he is far gone, far gone: and
truly in my youth I suffered much extremity for
love; very near this. I'll speak to him again.
What do you read, my lord?

HAMLET

Words, words, words.

LORD POLONIUS

What is the matter, my lord?

HAMLET

Between who?

LORD POLONIUS

I mean, the matter that you read, my lord.

HAMLET

Slanders, sir: for the satirical rogue says here
that old men have grey beards, that their faces are
wrinkled, their eyes purging thick amber and
plum-tree gum and that they have a plentiful lack of
wit, together with most weak hams: all which, sir,
though I most powerfully and potently believe, yet
I hold it not honesty to have it thus set down, for
yourself, sir, should be old as I am, if like a crab
you could go backward.

LORD POLONIUS

[Aside] Though this be madness, yet there is method
in 't. Will you walk out of the air, my lord?

HAMLET

Into my grave.

LORD POLONIUS

Indeed, that is out o' the air.

Aside

How pregnant sometimes his replies are! a happiness
that often madness hits on, which reason and sanity
could not so prosperously be delivered of. I will
leave him, and suddenly contrive the means of
meeting between him and my daughter.--My honourable
lord, I will most humbly take my leave of you.

HAMLET

You cannot, sir, take from me any thing that I will
more willingly part withal: except my life, except
my life, except my life.

LORD POLONIUS
  Fare you well, my lord.
HAMLET
  These tedious old fools!

Enter ROSENCRANTZ and GUILDENSTERN

LORD POLONIUS
  You go to seek the Lord Hamlet; there he is.
ROSENCRANTZ
  [To POLONIUS] God save you, sir!

Exit POLONIUS

GUILDENSTERN
  My honoured lord!
ROSENCRANTZ
  My most dear lord!
HAMLET
  My excellent good friends! How dost thou,
  Guildenstern? Ah, Rosencrantz! Good lads, how do ye
  both?
ROSENCRANTZ
  As the indifferent children of the earth.
GUILDENSTERN
  Happy, in that we are not over-happy;
  On fortune's cap we are not the very button.
HAMLET
  Nor the soles of her shoe?
ROSENCRANTZ
  Neither, my lord.
HAMLET
  Then you live about her waist, or in the middle of
  her favours?
GUILDENSTERN

'Faith, her privates we.
HAMLET

In the secret parts of fortune? O, most true; she
is a strumpet. What's the news?

ROSENCRANTZ

None, my lord, but that the world's grown honest.

HAMLET

Then is doomsday near: but your news is not true.
Let me question more in particular: what have you,
my good friends, deserved at the hands of fortune,
that she sends you to prison hither?

GUILDENSTERN

Prison, my lord!

HAMLET

Denmark's a prison.

ROSENCRANTZ

Then is the world one.

HAMLET

A goodly one; in which there are many confines,
wards and dungeons, Denmark being one o' the worst.

ROSENCRANTZ

We think not so, my lord.

HAMLET

Why, then, 'tis none to you; for there is nothing
either good or bad, but thinking makes it so: to me
it is a prison.

ROSENCRANTZ

Why then, your ambition makes it one; 'tis too
narrow for your mind.

HAMLET

O God, I could be bounded in a nut shell and count
myself a king of infinite space, were it not that I
have bad dreams.

GUILDENSTERN

Which dreams indeed are ambition, for the very
substance of the ambitious is merely the shadow of a
dream.

HAMLET

A dream itself is but a shadow.

ROSENCRANTZ

Truly, and I hold ambition of so airy and light a
quality that it is but a shadow's shadow.

HAMLET

Then are our beggars bodies, and our monarchs and
outstretched heroes the beggars' shadows. Shall we
to the court? for, by my fay, I cannot reason.

ROSENCRANTZ GUILDENSTERN

We'll wait upon you.

HAMLET

No such matter: I will not sort you with the rest
of my servants, for, to speak to you like an honest
man, I am most dreadfully attended. But, in the
beaten way of friendship, what make you at Elsinore?

ROSENCRANTZ

To visit you, my lord; no other occasion.

HAMLET

Beggar that I am, I am even poor in thanks; but I
thank you: and sure, dear friends, my thanks are
too dear a halfpenny. Were you not sent for? Is it
your own inclining? Is it a free visitation? Come,
deal justly with me: come, come; nay, speak.

GUILDENSTERN

What should we say, my lord?

HAMLET

Why, any thing, but to the purpose. You were sent
for; and there is a kind of confession in your looks
which your modesties have not craft enough to colour:
I know the good king and queen have sent for you.

ROSENCRANTZ

To what end, my lord?

HAMLET

That you must teach me. But let me conjure you, by
the rights of our fellowship, by the consonancy of
our youth, by the obligation of our ever-preserved
love, and by what more dear a better proposer could
charge you withal, be even and direct with me,
whether you were sent for, or no?

ROSENCRANTZ

[Aside to GUILDENSTERN] What say you?

HAMLET

[Aside] Nay, then, I have an eye of you.--If you
love me, hold not off.

GUILDENSTERN

My lord, we were sent for.

HAMLET

I will tell you why; so shall my anticipation
prevent your discovery, and your secrecy to the king
and queen moult no feather. I have of late--but
wherefore I know not--lost all my mirth, forgone all
custom of exercises; and indeed it goes so heavily
with my disposition that this goodly frame, the
earth, seems to me a sterile promontory, this most
excellent canopy, the air, look you, this brave
o'erhanging firmament, this majestical roof fretted
with golden fire, why, it appears no other thing to
me than a foul and pestilent congregation of vapours.
What a piece of work is a man! how noble in reason!
how infinite in faculty! in form and moving how
express and admirable! in action how like an angel!
in apprehension how like a god! the beauty of the
world! the paragon of animals! And yet, to me,
what is this quintessence of dust? man delights not

me: no, nor woman neither, though by your smiling
you seem to say so.

ROSENCRANTZ

My lord, there was no such stuff in my thoughts.

HAMLET

Why did you laugh then, when I said 'man delights not
me'?

ROSENCRANTZ

To think, my lord, if you delight not in man, what
lenten entertainment the players shall receive from
you: we coted them on the way; and hither are they
coming, to offer you service.

HAMLET

He that plays the king shall be welcome; his majesty
shall have tribute of me; the adventurous knight
shall use his foil and target; the lover shall not
sigh gratis; the humourous man shall end his part
in peace; the clown shall make those laugh whose
lungs are tickled o' the sere; and the lady shall
say her mind freely, or the blank verse shall halt
for't. What players are they?

ROSENCRANTZ

Even those you were wont to take delight in, the
tragedians of the city.

HAMLET

How chances it they travel? their residence, both
in reputation and profit, was better both ways.

ROSENCRANTZ

I think their inhibition comes by the means of the
late innovation.

HAMLET

Do they hold the same estimation they did when I was
in the city? are they so followed?

ROSENCRANTZ

No, indeed, are they not.

HAMLET

How comes it? do they grow rusty?

ROSENCRANTZ

Nay, their endeavour keeps in the wonted pace: but
there is, sir, an aery of children, little eyases,
that cry out on the top of question, and are most
tyrannically clapped for't: these are now the
fashion, and so berattle the common stages--so they
call them--that many wearing rapiers are afraid of
goose-quills and dare scarce come thither.

HAMLET

What, are they children? who maintains 'em? how are
they escoted? Will they pursue the quality no
longer than they can sing? will they not say
afterwards, if they should grow themselves to common
players--as it is most like, if their means are no
better--their writers do them wrong, to make them
exclaim against their own succession?

ROSENCRANTZ

'Faith, there has been much to do on both sides; and
the nation holds it no sin to tarre them to
controversy: there was, for a while, no money bid
for argument, unless the poet and the player went to
cuffs in the question.

HAMLET

Is't possible?

GUILDENSTERN

O, there has been much throwing about of brains.

HAMLET

Do the boys carry it away?

ROSENCRANTZ

Ay, that they do, my lord; Hercules and his load too.

HAMLET

It is not very strange; for mine uncle is king of
Denmark, and those that would make mows at him
while
my father lived, give twenty, forty, fifty, an
hundred ducats a-piece for his picture in little.
'Sblood, there is something in this more than
natural, if philosophy could find it out.

Flourish of trumpets within

GUILDENSTERN
There are the players.
HAMLET
Gentlemen, you are welcome to Elsinore. Your hands,
come then: the appurtenance of welcome is fashion
and ceremony: let me comply with you in this garb,
lest my extent to the players, which, I tell you,
must show fairly outward, should more appear like
entertainment than yours. You are welcome: but my
uncle-father and aunt-mother are deceived.
GUILDENSTERN
In what, my dear lord?
HAMLET
I am but mad north-north-west: when the wind is
southerly I know a hawk from a handsaw.

Enter POLONIUS

LORD POLONIUS
Well be with you, gentlemen!
HAMLET
Hark you, Guildenstern; and you too: at each ear a
hearer: that great baby you see there is not yet
out of his swaddling-clouts.
ROSENCRANTZ

Happily he's the second time come to them; for they
say an old man is twice a child.

HAMLET

I will prophesy he comes to tell me of the players;
mark it. You say right, sir: o' Monday morning;
'twas so indeed.

LORD POLONIUS

My lord, I have news to tell you.

HAMLET

My lord, I have news to tell you.
When Roscius was an actor in Rome,--

LORD POLONIUS

The actors are come hither, my lord.

HAMLET

Buz, buz!

LORD POLONIUS

Upon mine honour,--

HAMLET

Then came each actor on his ass,--

LORD POLONIUS

The best actors in the world, either for tragedy,
comedy, history, pastoral, pastoral-comical,
historical-pastoral, tragical-historical, tragical-
comical-historical-pastoral, scene individable, or
poem unlimited: Seneca cannot be too heavy, nor
Plautus too light. For the law of writ and the
liberty, these are the only men.

HAMLET

O Jephthah, judge of Israel, what a treasure hadst thou!

LORD POLONIUS

What a treasure had he, my lord?

HAMLET

Why,
'One fair daughter and no more,

The which he loved passing well.'
LORD POLONIUS
   [Aside] Still on my daughter.
HAMLET
   Am I not i' the right, old Jephthah?
LORD POLONIUS
   If you call me Jephthah, my lord, I have a daughter
   that I love passing well.
HAMLET
   Nay, that follows not.
LORD POLONIUS
   What follows, then, my lord?
HAMLET
   Why,
   'As by lot, God wot,'
   and then, you know,
   'It came to pass, as most like it was,'--
   the first row of the pious chanson will show you
   more; for look, where my abridgement comes.

Enter four or five Players

You are welcome, masters; welcome, all. I am glad
to see thee well. Welcome, good friends. O, my old
friend! thy face is valenced since I saw thee last:
comest thou to beard me in Denmark? What, my young
lady and mistress! By'r lady, your ladyship is
nearer to heaven than when I saw you last, by the
altitude of a chopine. Pray God, your voice, like
apiece of uncurrent gold, be not cracked within the
ring. Masters, you are all welcome. We'll e'en
to't like French falconers, fly at any thing we see:
we'll have a speech straight: come, give us a taste
of your quality; come, a passionate speech.
First Player

66

What speech, my lord?
HAMLET
> I heard thee speak me a speech once, but it was
> never acted; or, if it was, not above once; for the
> play, I remember, pleased not the million; 'twas
> caviare to the general: but it was--as I received
> it, and others, whose judgments in such matters
> cried in the top of mine--an excellent play, well
> digested in the scenes, set down with as much
> modesty as cunning. I remember, one said there
> were no sallets in the lines to make the matter
> savoury, nor no matter in the phrase that might
> indict the author of affectation; but called it an
> honest method, as wholesome as sweet, and by very
> much more handsome than fine. One speech in it I
> chiefly loved: 'twas Aeneas' tale to Dido; and
> thereabout of it especially, where he speaks of
> Priam's slaughter: if it live in your memory, begin
> at this line: let me see, let me see--
> 'The rugged Pyrrhus, like the Hyrcanian beast,'--
> it is not so:--it begins with Pyrrhus:--
> 'The rugged Pyrrhus, he whose sable arms,
> Black as his purpose, did the night resemble
> When he lay couched in the ominous horse,
> Hath now this dread and black complexion smear'd
> With heraldry more dismal; head to foot
> Now is he total gules; horridly trick'd
> With blood of fathers, mothers, daughters, sons,
> Baked and impasted with the parching streets,
> That lend a tyrannous and damned light
> To their lord's murder: roasted in wrath and fire,
> And thus o'er-sized with coagulate gore,
> With eyes like carbuncles, the hellish Pyrrhus
> Old grandsire Priam seeks.'

So, proceed you.

LORD POLONIUS

'Fore God, my lord, well spoken, with good accent and
good discretion.

First Player

'Anon he finds him
Striking too short at Greeks; his antique sword,
Rebellious to his arm, lies where it falls,
Repugnant to command: unequal match'd,
Pyrrhus at Priam drives; in rage strikes wide;
But with the whiff and wind of his fell sword
The unnerved father falls. Then senseless Ilium,
Seeming to feel this blow, with flaming top
Stoops to his base, and with a hideous crash
Takes prisoner Pyrrhus' ear: for, lo! his sword,
Which was declining on the milky head
Of reverend Priam, seem'd i' the air to stick:
So, as a painted tyrant, Pyrrhus stood,
And like a neutral to his will and matter,
Did nothing.
But, as we often see, against some storm,
A silence in the heavens, the rack stand still,
The bold winds speechless and the orb below
As hush as death, anon the dreadful thunder
Doth rend the region, so, after Pyrrhus' pause,
Aroused vengeance sets him new a-work;
And never did the Cyclops' hammers fall
On Mars's armour forged for proof eterne
With less remorse than Pyrrhus' bleeding sword
Now falls on Priam.
Out, out, thou strumpet, Fortune! All you gods,
In general synod 'take away her power;
Break all the spokes and fellies from her wheel,
And bowl the round nave down the hill of heaven,

As low as to the fiends!'
LORD POLONIUS
This is too long.
HAMLET
It shall to the barber's, with your beard. Prithee,
say on: he's for a jig or a tale of bawdry, or he
sleeps: say on: come to Hecuba.
First Player
'But who, O, who had seen the mobled queen--'
HAMLET
'The mobled queen?'
LORD POLONIUS
That's good; 'mobled queen' is good.
First Player
'Run barefoot up and down, threatening the flames
With bisson rheum; a clout upon that head
Where late the diadem stood, and for a robe,
About her lank and all o'er-teemed loins,
A blanket, in the alarm of fear caught up;
Who this had seen, with tongue in venom steep'd,
'Gainst Fortune's state would treason have
pronounced:
But if the gods themselves did see her then
When she saw Pyrrhus make malicious sport
In mincing with his sword her husband's limbs,
The instant burst of clamour that she made,
Unless things mortal move them not at all,
Would have made milch the burning eyes of heaven,
And passion in the gods.'
LORD POLONIUS
Look, whether he has not turned his colour and has
tears in's eyes. Pray you, no more.
HAMLET
'Tis well: I'll have thee speak out the rest soon.

Good my lord, will you see the players well
bestowed? Do you hear, let them be well used; for
they are the abstract and brief chronicles of the
time: after your death you were better have a bad
epitaph than their ill report while you live.

LORD POLONIUS

My lord, I will use them according to their desert.

HAMLET

God's bodykins, man, much better: use every man
after his desert, and who should 'scape whipping?
Use them after your own honour and dignity: the less
they deserve, the more merit is in your bounty.
Take them in.

LORD POLONIUS

Come, sirs.

HAMLET

Follow him, friends: we'll hear a play to-morrow.

Exit POLONIUS with all the Players but the First

Dost thou hear me, old friend; can you play the
Murder of Gonzago?

First Player

Ay, my lord.

HAMLET

We'll ha't to-morrow night. You could, for a need,
study a speech of some dozen or sixteen lines, which
I would set down and insert in't, could you not?

First Player

Ay, my lord.

HAMLET

Very well. Follow that lord; and look you mock him
not.

Exit First Player

My good friends, I'll leave you till night: you are
welcome to Elsinore.
ROSENCRANTZ
Good my lord!
HAMLET
Ay, so, God be wi' ye;

Exeunt ROSENCRANTZ and GUILDENSTERN
Now I am alone.
O, what a rogue and peasant slave am I!
Is it not monstrous that this player here,
But in a fiction, in a dream of passion,
Could force his soul so to his own conceit
That from her working all his visage wann'd,
Tears in his eyes, distraction in's aspect,
A broken voice, and his whole function suiting
With forms to his conceit? and all for nothing!
For Hecuba!
What's Hecuba to him, or he to Hecuba,
That he should weep for her? What would he do,
Had he the motive and the cue for passion
That I have? He would drown the stage with tears
And cleave the general ear with horrid speech,
Make mad the guilty and appal the free,
Confound the ignorant, and amaze indeed
The very faculties of eyes and ears. Yet I,
A dull and muddy-mettled rascal, peak,
Like John-a-dreams, unpregnant of my cause,
And can say nothing; no, not for a king,
Upon whose property and most dear life
A damn'd defeat was made. Am I a coward?
Who calls me villain? breaks my pate across?
Plucks off my beard, and blows it in my face?
Tweaks me by the nose? gives me the lie i' the throat,

As deep as to the lungs? who does me this?
Ha!
'Swounds, I should take it: for it cannot be
But I am pigeon-liver'd and lack gall
To make oppression bitter, or ere this
I should have fatted all the region kites
With this slave's offal: bloody, bawdy villain!
Remorseless, treacherous, lecherous, kindless villain!
O, vengeance!
Why, what an ass am I! This is most brave,
That I, the son of a dear father murder'd,
Prompted to my revenge by heaven and hell,
Must, like a whore, unpack my heart with words,
And fall a-cursing, like a very drab,
A scullion!
Fie upon't! foh! About, my brain! I have heard
That guilty creatures sitting at a play
Have by the very cunning of the scene
Been struck so to the soul that presently
They have proclaim'd their malefactions;
For murder, though it have no tongue, will speak
With most miraculous organ. I'll have these players
Play something like the murder of my father
Before mine uncle: I'll observe his looks;
I'll tent him to the quick: if he but blench,
I know my course. The spirit that I have seen
May be the devil: and the devil hath power
To assume a pleasing shape; yea, and perhaps
Out of my weakness and my melancholy,
As he is very potent with such spirits,
Abuses me to damn me: I'll have grounds
More relative than this: the play 's the thing
Wherein I'll catch the conscience of the king.

Exit

ACT III

SCENE I.

A room in the castle.

Enter KING CLAUDIUS, QUEEN GERTRUDE, POLONIUS, OPHELIA, ROSENCRANTZ, and GUILDENSTERN

KING CLAUDIUS
And can you, by no drift of circumstance,
Get from him why he puts on this confusion,
Grating so harshly all his days of quiet
With turbulent and dangerous lunacy?

ROSENCRANTZ
He does confess he feels himself distracted;
But from what cause he will by no means speak.

GUILDENSTERN
Nor do we find him forward to be sounded,
But, with a crafty madness, keeps aloof,
When we would bring him on to some confession
Of his true state.

QUEEN GERTRUDE
Did he receive you well?

ROSENCRANTZ
Most like a gentleman.

GUILDENSTERN
But with much forcing of his disposition.

ROSENCRANTZ
Niggard of question; but, of our demands,
Most free in his reply.

QUEEN GERTRUDE
Did you assay him?
To any pastime?

ROSENCRANTZ
 Madam, it so fell out, that certain players
 We o'er-raught on the way: of these we told him;
 And there did seem in him a kind of joy
 To hear of it: they are about the court,
 And, as I think, they have already order
 This night to play before him.
LORD POLONIUS
 'Tis most true:
 And he beseech'd me to entreat your majesties
 To hear and see the matter.
KING CLAUDIUS
 With all my heart; and it doth much content me
 To hear him so inclined.
 Good gentlemen, give him a further edge,
 And drive his purpose on to these delights.
ROSENCRANTZ
 We shall, my lord.

    Exeunt ROSENCRANTZ and GUILDENSTERN

KING CLAUDIUS
 Sweet Gertrude, leave us too;
 For we have closely sent for Hamlet hither,
 That he, as 'twere by accident, may here
 Affront Ophelia:
 Her father and myself, lawful espials,
 Will so bestow ourselves that, seeing, unseen,
 We may of their encounter frankly judge,
 And gather by him, as he is behaved,
 If 't be the affliction of his love or no
 That thus he suffers for.
QUEEN GERTRUDE
 I shall obey you.
 And for your part, Ophelia, I do wish

That your good beauties be the happy cause
Of Hamlet's wildness: so shall I hope your virtues
Will bring him to his wonted way again,
To both your honours.

OPHELIA

Madam, I wish it may.

Exit QUEEN GERTRUDE

LORD POLONIUS

Ophelia, walk you here. Gracious, so please you,
We will bestow ourselves.

To OPHELIA

Read on this book;
That show of such an exercise may colour
Your loneliness. We are oft to blame in this,--
'Tis too much proved--that with devotion's visage
And pious action we do sugar o'er
The devil himself.

KING CLAUDIUS

[Aside] O, 'tis too true!
How smart a lash that speech doth give my conscience!
The harlot's cheek, beautied with plastering art,
Is not more ugly to the thing that helps it
Than is my deed to my most painted word:
O heavy burthen!

LORD POLONIUS

I hear him coming: let's withdraw, my lord.

Exeunt KING CLAUDIUS and POLONIUS

Enter HAMLET

HAMLET

To be, or not to be, that is the question,
Whether 'tis nobler in the mind to suffer
The slings and arrows of outrageous fortune,
Or to take arms against a sea of troubles,
And by opposing end them? To die: to sleep;
No more; and by a sleep to say we end
The heart-ache and the thousand natural shocks
That flesh is heir to, 'tis a consummation
Devoutly to be wish'd. To die, to sleep;
To sleep: perchance to dream: ay, there's the rub;
For in that sleep of death what dreams may come
When we have shuffled off this mortal coil,
Must give us pause: there's the respect
That makes calamity of so long life;
For who would bear the whips and scorns of time,
The oppressor's wrong, the proud man's contumely,
The pangs of despised love, the law's delay,
The insolence of office and the spurns
That patient merit of the unworthy takes,
When he himself might his quietus make
With a bare bodkin? who would fardels bear,
To grunt and sweat under a weary life,
But that the dread of something after death,
The undiscover'd country from whose bourn
No traveller returns, puzzles the will
And makes us rather bear those ills we have
Than fly to others that we know not of?
Thus conscience does make cowards of us all;
And thus the native hue of resolution
Is sicklied o'er with the pale cast of thought,
And enterprises of great pith and moment
With this regard their currents turn awry,
And lose the name of action.--Soft you now!
The fair Ophelia! Nymph, in thy orisons

Be all my sins remember'd.

OPHELIA

Good my lord,
How does your honour for this many a day?

HAMLET

I humbly thank you; well, well, well.

OPHELIA

My lord, I have remembrances of yours,
That I have longed long to re-deliver;
I pray you, now receive them.

HAMLET

No, not I;
I never gave you aught.

OPHELIA

My honour'd lord, you know right well you did;
And, with them, words of so sweet breath composed
As made the things more rich: their perfume lost,
Take these again; for to the noble mind
Rich gifts wax poor when givers prove unkind.
There, my lord.

HAMLET

Ha, ha! are you honest?

OPHELIA

My lord?

HAMLET

Are you fair?

OPHELIA

What means your lordship?

HAMLET

That if you be honest and fair, your honesty should
admit no discourse to your beauty.

OPHELIA

Could beauty, my lord, have better commerce than
with honesty?

HAMLET

Ay, truly; for the power of beauty will sooner
transform honesty from what it is to a bawd than the
force of honesty can translate beauty into his
likeness: this was sometime a paradox, but now the
time gives it proof. I did love you once.

OPHELIA

Indeed, my lord, you made me believe so.

HAMLET

You should not have believed me; for virtue cannot
so inoculate our old stock but we shall relish of
it: I loved you not.

OPHELIA

I was the more deceived.

HAMLET

Get thee to a nunnery: why wouldst thou be a
breeder of sinners? I am myself indifferent honest;
but yet I could accuse me of such things that it
were better my mother had not borne me: I am very
proud, revengeful, ambitious, with more offences at
my beck than I have thoughts to put them in,
imagination to give them shape, or time to act them
in. What should such fellows as I do crawling
between earth and heaven? We are arrant knaves,
all; believe none of us. Go thy ways to a nunnery.
Where's your father?

OPHELIA

At home, my lord.

HAMLET

Let the doors be shut upon him, that he may play the
fool no where but in's own house. Farewell.

OPHELIA

O, help him, you sweet heavens!

HAMLET

If thou dost marry, I'll give thee this plague for
thy dowry: be thou as chaste as ice, as pure as
snow, thou shalt not escape calumny. Get thee to a
nunnery, go: farewell. Or, if thou wilt needs
marry, marry a fool; for wise men know well enough
what monsters you make of them. To a nunnery, go,
and quickly too. Farewell.

OPHELIA

O heavenly powers, restore him!

HAMLET

I have heard of your paintings too, well enough; God
has given you one face, and you make yourselves
another: you jig, you amble, and you lisp, and
nick-name God's creatures, and make your wantonness
your ignorance. Go to, I'll no more on't; it hath
made me mad. I say, we will have no more marriages:
those that are married already, all but one, shall
live; the rest shall keep as they are. To a
nunnery, go.

Exit

OPHELIA

O, what a noble mind is here o'erthrown!
The courtier's, soldier's, scholar's, eye, tongue, sword;
The expectancy and rose of the fair state,
The glass of fashion and the mould of form,
The observed of all observers, quite, quite down!
And I, of ladies most deject and wretched,
That suck'd the honey of his music vows,
Now see that noble and most sovereign reason,
Like sweet bells jangled, out of tune and harsh;
That unmatch'd form and feature of blown youth
Blasted with ecstasy: O, woe is me,
To have seen what I have seen, see what I see!

Re-enter KING CLAUDIUS and POLONIUS

KING CLAUDIUS
    Love! his affections do not that way tend;
    Nor what he spake, though it lack'd form a little,
    Was not like madness. There's something in his soul,
    O'er which his melancholy sits on brood;
    And I do doubt the hatch and the disclose
    Will be some danger: which for to prevent,
    I have in quick determination
    Thus set it down: he shall with speed to England,
    For the demand of our neglected tribute
    Haply the seas and countries different
    With variable objects shall expel
    This something-settled matter in his heart,
    Whereon his brains still beating puts him thus
    From fashion of himself. What think you on't?
LORD POLONIUS
    It shall do well: but yet do I believe
    The origin and commencement of his grief
    Sprung from neglected love. How now, Ophelia!
    You need not tell us what Lord Hamlet said;
    We heard it all. My lord, do as you please;
    But, if you hold it fit, after the play
    Let his queen mother all alone entreat him
    To show his grief: let her be round with him;
    And I'll be placed, so please you, in the ear
    Of all their conference. If she find him not,
    To England send him, or confine him where
    Your wisdom best shall think.
KING CLAUDIUS
    It shall be so:
    Madness in great ones must not unwatch'd go.

Exeunt

SCENE II.

A hall in the castle.

Enter HAMLET and Players

HAMLET

Speak the speech, I pray you, as I pronounced it to
you, trippingly on the tongue: but if you mouth it,
as many of your players do, I had as lief the
town-crier spoke my lines. Nor do not saw the air
too much with your hand, thus, but use all gently;
for in the very torrent, tempest, and, as I may say,
the whirlwind of passion, you must acquire and beget
a temperance that may give it smoothness. O, it
offends me to the soul to hear a robustious
periwig-pated fellow tear a passion to tatters, to
very rags, to split the ears of the groundlings, who
for the most part are capable of nothing but
inexplicable dumbshows and noise: I would have such
a fellow whipped for o'erdoing Termagant; it
out-herods Herod: pray you, avoid it.

First Player

I warrant your honour.

HAMLET

Be not too tame neither, but let your own discretion
be your tutor: suit the action to the word, the
word to the action; with this special o'erstep not
the modesty of nature: for any thing so overdone is
from the purpose of playing, whose end, both at the
first and now, was and is, to hold, as 'twere, the
mirror up to nature; to show virtue her own feature,
scorn her own image, and the very age and body of
the time his form and pressure. Now this overdone,

or come tardy off, though it make the unskilful
laugh, cannot but make the judicious grieve; the
censure of the which one must in your allowance
o'erweigh a whole theatre of others. O, there be
players that I have seen play, and heard others
praise, and that highly, not to speak it profanely,
that, neither having the accent of Christians nor
the gait of Christian, pagan, nor man, have so
strutted and bellowed that I have thought some of
nature's journeymen had made men and not made them
well, they imitated humanity so abominably.

First Player

I hope we have reformed that indifferently with us,
sir.

HAMLET

O, reform it altogether. And let those that play
your clowns speak no more than is set down for them;
for there be of them that will themselves laugh, to
set on some quantity of barren spectators to laugh
too; though, in the mean time, some necessary
question of the play be then to be considered:
that's villanous, and shows a most pitiful ambition
in the fool that uses it. Go, make you ready.

Exeunt Players

Enter POLONIUS, ROSENCRANTZ, and GUILDENSTERN

How now, my lord! I will the king hear this piece of
work?

LORD POLONIUS

And the queen too, and that presently.

HAMLET

Bid the players make haste.

Exit POLONIUS

Will you two help to hasten them?
ROSENCRANTZ GUILDENSTERN
  We will, my lord.

Exeunt ROSENCRANTZ and GUILDENSTERN

HAMLET
  What ho! Horatio!

Enter HORATIO

HORATIO
  Here, sweet lord, at your service.
HAMLET
  Horatio, thou art e'en as just a man
  As e'er my conversation coped withal.
HORATIO
  O, my dear lord,--
HAMLET
  Nay, do not think I flatter;
  For what advancement may I hope from thee
  That no revenue hast but thy good spirits,
  To feed and clothe thee? Why should the poor be
  flatter'd?
  No, let the candied tongue lick absurd pomp,
  And crook the pregnant hinges of the knee
  Where thrift may follow fawning. Dost thou hear?
  Since my dear soul was mistress of her choice
  And could of men distinguish, her election
  Hath seal'd thee for herself; for thou hast been
  As one, in suffering all, that suffers nothing,
  A man that fortune's buffets and rewards
  Hast ta'en with equal thanks: and blest are those

Whose blood and judgment are so well commingled,
That they are not a pipe for fortune's finger
To sound what stop she please. Give me that man
That is not passion's slave, and I will wear him
In my heart's core, ay, in my heart of heart,
As I do thee.--Something too much of this.--
There is a play to-night before the king;
One scene of it comes near the circumstance
Which I have told thee of my father's death:
I prithee, when thou seest that act afoot,
Even with the very comment of thy soul
Observe mine uncle: if his occulted guilt
Do not itself unkennel in one speech,
It is a damned ghost that we have seen,
And my imaginations are as foul
As Vulcan's stithy. Give him heedful note;
For I mine eyes will rivet to his face,
And after we will both our judgments join
In censure of his seeming.

HORATIO
    Well, my lord:
    If he steal aught the whilst this play is playing,
    And 'scape detecting, I will pay the theft.

HAMLET
    They are coming to the play; I must be idle:
    Get you a place.

*Danish march. A flourish. Enter KING CLAUDIUS, QUEEN
    GERTRUDE, POLONIUS, OPHELIA, ROSENCRANTZ,
    GUILDENSTERN, and others*

KING CLAUDIUS
    How fares our cousin Hamlet?

HAMLET
    Excellent, i' faith; of the chameleon's dish: I eat

the air, promise-crammed: you cannot feed capons so.

KING CLAUDIUS

I have nothing with this answer, Hamlet; these words
are not mine.

HAMLET

No, nor mine now.

To POLONIUS

My lord, you played once i' the university, you say?

LORD POLONIUS

That did I, my lord; and was accounted a good actor.

HAMLET

What did you enact?

LORD POLONIUS

I did enact Julius Caesar: I was killed i' the
Capitol; Brutus killed me.

HAMLET

It was a brute part of him to kill so capital a calf
there. Be the players ready?

ROSENCRANTZ

Ay, my lord; they stay upon your patience.

QUEEN GERTRUDE

Come hither, my dear Hamlet, sit by me.

HAMLET

No, good mother, here's metal more attractive.

LORD POLONIUS

[To KING CLAUDIUS] O, ho! do you mark that?

HAMLET

Lady, shall I lie in your lap?

Lying down at OPHELIA's feet

OPHELIA

No, my lord.

HAMLET
  I mean, my head upon your lap?
OPHELIA
  Ay, my lord.
HAMLET
  Do you think I meant country matters?
OPHELIA
  I think nothing, my lord.
HAMLET
  That's a fair thought to lie between maids' legs.
OPHELIA
  What is, my lord?
HAMLET
  Nothing.
OPHELIA
  You are merry, my lord.
HAMLET
  Who, I?
OPHELIA
  Ay, my lord.
HAMLET
  O God, your only jig-maker. What should a man do
  but be merry? for, look you, how cheerfully my
  mother looks, and my father died within these two
  hours.
OPHELIA
  Nay, 'tis twice two months, my lord.
HAMLET
  So long? Nay then, let the devil wear black, for
  I'll have a suit of sables. O heavens! die two
  months ago, and not forgotten yet? Then there's
  hope a great man's memory may outlive his life half
  a year: but, by'r lady, he must build churches,
  then; or else shall he suffer not thinking on, with

the hobby-horse, whose epitaph is 'For, O, for, O, the hobby-horse is forgot.'

Hautboys play. The dumb-show enters

Enter a King and a Queen very lovingly; the Queen embracing him, and he her. She kneels, and makes show of protestation unto him. He takes her up, and declines his head upon her neck: lays him down upon a bank of flowers: she, seeing him asleep, leaves him. Anon comes in a fellow, takes off his crown, kisses it, and pours poison in the King's ears, and exit. The Queen returns; finds the King dead, and makes passionate action. The Poisoner, with some two or three Mutes, comes in again, seeming to lament with her. The dead body is carried away. The Poisoner wooes the Queen with gifts: she seems loath and unwilling awhile, but in the end accepts his love

Exeunt

OPHELIA
  What means this, my lord?
HAMLET
  Marry, this is miching mallecho; it means mischief.
OPHELIA
  Belike this show imports the argument of the play.

Enter Prologue

HAMLET
  We shall know by this fellow: the players cannot keep counsel; they'll tell all.
OPHELIA
  Will he tell us what this show meant?

HAMLET

Ay, or any show that you'll show him: be not you ashamed to show, he'll not shame to tell you what it means.

OPHELIA

You are naught, you are naught: I'll mark the play.

Prologue

For us, and for our tragedy,
Here stooping to your clemency,
We beg your hearing patiently.

Exit

HAMLET

Is this a prologue, or the posy of a ring?

OPHELIA

'Tis brief, my lord.

HAMLET

As woman's love.

Enter two Players, King and Queen

Player King

Full thirty times hath Phoebus' cart gone round
Neptune's salt wash and Tellus' orbed ground,
And thirty dozen moons with borrow'd sheen
About the world have times twelve thirties been,
Since love our hearts and Hymen did our hands
Unite commutual in most sacred bands.

Player Queen

So many journeys may the sun and moon
Make us again count o'er ere love be done!
But, woe is me, you are so sick of late,
So far from cheer and from your former state,
That I distrust you. Yet, though I distrust,

Discomfort you, my lord, it nothing must:
For women's fear and love holds quantity;
In neither aught, or in extremity.
Now, what my love is, proof hath made you know;
And as my love is sized, my fear is so:
Where love is great, the littlest doubts are fear;
Where little fears grow great, great love grows there.
Player King
   'Faith, I must leave thee, love, and shortly too;
   My operant powers their functions leave to do:
   And thou shalt live in this fair world behind,
   Honour'd, beloved; and haply one as kind
   For husband shalt thou--
Player Queen
   O, confound the rest!
   Such love must needs be treason in my breast:
   In second husband let me be accurst!
   None wed the second but who kill'd the first.
HAMLET
   [Aside] Wormwood, wormwood.
Player Queen
   The instances that second marriage move
   Are base respects of thrift, but none of love:
   A second time I kill my husband dead,
   When second husband kisses me in bed.
Player King
   I do believe you think what now you speak;
   But what we do determine oft we break.
   Purpose is but the slave to memory,
   Of violent birth, but poor validity;
   Which now, like fruit unripe, sticks on the tree;
   But fall, unshaken, when they mellow be.
   Most necessary 'tis that we forget
   To pay ourselves what to ourselves is debt:

What to ourselves in passion we propose,
The passion ending, doth the purpose lose.
The violence of either grief or joy
Their own enactures with themselves destroy:
Where joy most revels, grief doth most lament;
Grief joys, joy grieves, on slender accident.
This world is not for aye, nor 'tis not strange
That even our loves should with our fortunes change;
For 'tis a question left us yet to prove,
Whether love lead fortune, or else fortune love.
The great man down, you mark his favourite flies;
The poor advanced makes friends of enemies.
And hitherto doth love on fortune tend;
For who not needs shall never lack a friend,
And who in want a hollow friend doth try,
Directly seasons him his enemy.
But, orderly to end where I begun,
Our wills and fates do so contrary run
That our devices still are overthrown;
Our thoughts are ours, their ends none of our own:
So think thou wilt no second husband wed;
But die thy thoughts when thy first lord is dead.

Player Queen
Nor earth to me give food, nor heaven light!
Sport and repose lock from me day and night!
To desperation turn my trust and hope!
An anchor's cheer in prison be my scope!
Each opposite that blanks the face of joy
Meet what I would have well and it destroy!
Both here and hence pursue me lasting strife,
If, once a widow, ever I be wife!

HAMLET
If she should break it now!

Player King

'Tis deeply sworn. Sweet, leave me here awhile;
My spirits grow dull, and fain I would beguile
The tedious day with sleep.

Sleeps

Player Queen
  Sleep rock thy brain,
  And never come mischance between us twain!

Exit

HAMLET
  Madam, how like you this play?
QUEEN GERTRUDE
  The lady protests too much, methinks.
HAMLET
  O, but she'll keep her word.
KING CLAUDIUS
  Have you heard the argument? Is there no offence in 't?
HAMLET
  No, no, they do but jest, poison in jest; no offence
  i' the world.
KING CLAUDIUS
  What do you call the play?
HAMLET
  The Mouse-trap. Marry, how? Tropically. This play
  is the image of a murder done in Vienna: Gonzago is
  the duke's name; his wife, Baptista: you shall see
  anon; 'tis a knavish piece of work: but what o'
  that? your majesty and we that have free souls, it
  touches us not: let the galled jade wince, our
  withers are unwrung.

Enter LUCIANUS

This is one Lucianus, nephew to the king.

OPHELIA

You are as good as a chorus, my lord.

HAMLET

I could interpret between you and your love, if I
could see the puppets dallying.

OPHELIA

You are keen, my lord, you are keen.

HAMLET

It would cost you a groaning to take off my edge.

OPHELIA

Still better, and worse.

HAMLET

So you must take your husbands. Begin, murderer;
pox, leave thy damnable faces, and begin. Come:
'the croaking raven doth bellow for revenge.'

LUCIANUS

Thoughts black, hands apt, drugs fit, and time agreeing;
Confederate season, else no creature seeing;
Thou mixture rank, of midnight weeds collected,
With Hecate's ban thrice blasted, thrice infected,
Thy natural magic and dire property,
On wholesome life usurp immediately.

Pours the poison into the sleeper's ears

HAMLET

He poisons him i' the garden for's estate. His
name's Gonzago: the story is extant, and writ in
choice Italian: you shall see anon how the murderer
gets the love of Gonzago's wife.

OPHELIA

The king rises.

HAMLET

What, frighted with false fire!

QUEEN GERTRUDE
  How fares my lord?
LORD POLONIUS
  Give o'er the play.
KING CLAUDIUS
  Give me some light: away!
All
  Lights, lights, lights!

Exeunt all but HAMLET and HORATIO

HAMLET
  Why, let the stricken deer go weep,
  The hart ungalled play;
  For some must watch, while some must sleep:
  So runs the world away.
  Would not this, sir, and a forest of feathers-- if
  the rest of my fortunes turn Turk with me--with two
  Provincial roses on my razed shoes, get me a
  fellowship in a cry of players, sir?
HORATIO
  Half a share.
HAMLET
  A whole one, I.
  For thou dost know, O Damon dear,
  This realm dismantled was
  Of Jove himself; and now reigns here
  A very, very--pajock.
HORATIO
  You might have rhymed.
HAMLET
  O good Horatio, I'll take the ghost's word for a
  thousand pound. Didst perceive?
HORATIO
  Very well, my lord.

HAMLET
  Upon the talk of the poisoning?
HORATIO
  I did very well note him.
HAMLET
  Ah, ha! Come, some music! come, the recorders!
  For if the king like not the comedy,
  Why then, belike, he likes it not, perdy.
  Come, some music!

  Re-enter ROSENCRANTZ and GUILDENSTERN

GUILDENSTERN
  Good my lord, vouchsafe me a word with you.
HAMLET
  Sir, a whole history.
GUILDENSTERN
  The king, sir,--
HAMLET
  Ay, sir, what of him?
GUILDENSTERN
  Is in his retirement marvellous distempered.
HAMLET
  With drink, sir?
GUILDENSTERN
  No, my lord, rather with choler.
HAMLET
  Your wisdom should show itself more richer to
  signify this to his doctor; for, for me to put him
  to his purgation would perhaps plunge him into far
  more choler.
GUILDENSTERN
  Good my lord, put your discourse into some frame and
  start not so wildly from my affair.
HAMLET

I am tame, sir: pronounce.

GUILDENSTERN

The queen, your mother, in most great affliction of spirit, hath sent me to you.

HAMLET

You are welcome.

GUILDENSTERN

Nay, good my lord, this courtesy is not of the right breed. If it shall please you to make me a wholesome answer, I will do your mother's commandment: if not, your pardon and my return shall be the end of my business.

HAMLET

Sir, I cannot.

GUILDENSTERN

What, my lord?

HAMLET

Make you a wholesome answer; my wit's diseased: but, sir, such answer as I can make, you shall command; or, rather, as you say, my mother: therefore no more, but to the matter: my mother, you say,--

ROSENCRANTZ

Then thus she says; your behavior hath struck her into amazement and admiration.

HAMLET

O wonderful son, that can so astonish a mother! But is there no sequel at the heels of this mother's admiration? Impart.

ROSENCRANTZ

She desires to speak with you in her closet, ere you go to bed.

HAMLET

We shall obey, were she ten times our mother. Have you any further trade with us?

ROSENCRANTZ

My lord, you once did love me.

HAMLET

So I do still, by these pickers and stealers.

ROSENCRANTZ

Good my lord, what is your cause of distemper? you
do, surely, bar the door upon your own liberty, if
you deny your griefs to your friend.

HAMLET

Sir, I lack advancement.

ROSENCRANTZ

How can that be, when you have the voice of the king
himself for your succession in Denmark?

HAMLET

Ay, but sir, 'While the grass grows,'--the proverb
is something musty.

Re-enter Players with recorders

O, the recorders! let me see one. To withdraw with
you:--why do you go about to recover the wind of me,
as if you would drive me into a toil?

GUILDENSTERN

O, my lord, if my duty be too bold, my love is too
unmannerly.

HAMLET

I do not well understand that. Will you play upon
this pipe?

GUILDENSTERN

My lord, I cannot.

HAMLET

I pray you.

GUILDENSTERN

Believe me, I cannot.

HAMLET

I do beseech you.
GUILDENSTERN
I know no touch of it, my lord.
HAMLET
'Tis as easy as lying: govern these ventages with
your lingers and thumb, give it breath with your
mouth, and it will discourse most eloquent music.
Look you, these are the stops.
GUILDENSTERN
But these cannot I command to any utterance of
harmony; I have not the skill.
HAMLET
Why, look you now, how unworthy a thing you make of
me! You would play upon me; you would seem to know
my stops; you would pluck out the heart of my
mystery; you would sound me from my lowest note to
the top of my compass: and there is much music,
excellent voice, in this little organ; yet cannot
you make it speak. 'Sblood, do you think I am
easier to be played on than a pipe? Call me what
instrument you will, though you can fret me, yet you
cannot play upon me.

Enter POLONIUS

God bless you, sir!
LORD POLONIUS
My lord, the queen would speak with you, and
presently.
HAMLET
Do you see yonder cloud that's almost in shape of a
camel?
LORD POLONIUS
By the mass, and 'tis like a camel, indeed.
HAMLET

Methinks it is like a weasel.
LORD POLONIUS
    It is backed like a weasel.
HAMLET
    Or like a whale?
LORD POLONIUS
    Very like a whale.
HAMLET
    Then I will come to my mother by and by. They fool
    me to the top of my bent. I will come by and by.
LORD POLONIUS
    I will say so.
HAMLET
    By and by is easily said.

Exit POLONIUS

Leave me, friends.

Exeunt all but HAMLET

Tis now the very witching time of night,
When churchyards yawn and hell itself breathes out
Contagion to this world: now could I drink hot blood,
And do such bitter business as the day
Would quake to look on. Soft! now to my mother.
O heart, lose not thy nature; let not ever
The soul of Nero enter this firm bosom:
Let me be cruel, not unnatural:
I will speak daggers to her, but use none;
My tongue and soul in this be hypocrites;
How in my words soever she be shent,
To give them seals never, my soul, consent!

Exit

SCENE III.

A room in the castle.

Enter KING CLAUDIUS, ROSENCRANTZ, and
GUILDENSTERN

KING CLAUDIUS
　　I like him not, nor stands it safe with us
　　To let his madness range. Therefore prepare you;
　　I your commission will forthwith dispatch,
　　And he to England shall along with you:
　　The terms of our estate may not endure
　　Hazard so dangerous as doth hourly grow
　　Out of his lunacies.
GUILDENSTERN
　　We will ourselves provide:
　　Most holy and religious fear it is
　　To keep those many many bodies safe
　　That live and feed upon your majesty.
ROSENCRANTZ
　　The single and peculiar life is bound,
　　With all the strength and armour of the mind,
　　To keep itself from noyance; but much more
　　That spirit upon whose weal depend and rest
　　The lives of many. The cease of majesty
　　Dies not alone; but, like a gulf, doth draw
　　What's near it with it: it is a massy wheel,
　　Fix'd on the summit of the highest mount,
　　To whose huge spokes ten thousand lesser things
　　Are mortised and adjoin'd; which, when it falls,
　　Each small annexment, petty consequence,
　　Attends the boisterous ruin. Never alone
　　Did the king sigh, but with a general groan.
KING CLAUDIUS
　　Arm you, I pray you, to this speedy voyage;

For we will fetters put upon this fear,
Which now goes too free-footed.
ROSENCRANTZ GUILDENSTERN
We will haste us.

Exeunt ROSENCRANTZ and GUILDENSTERN

Enter POLONIUS

LORD POLONIUS
My lord, he's going to his mother's closet:
Behind the arras I'll convey myself,
To hear the process; and warrant she'll tax him home:
And, as you said, and wisely was it said,
'Tis meet that some more audience than a mother,
Since nature makes them partial, should o'erhear
The speech, of vantage. Fare you well, my liege:
I'll call upon you ere you go to bed,
And tell you what I know.
KING CLAUDIUS
Thanks, dear my lord.

Exit POLONIUS

O, my offence is rank it smells to heaven;
It hath the primal eldest curse upon't,
A brother's murder. Pray can I not,
Though inclination be as sharp as will:
My stronger guilt defeats my strong intent;
And, like a man to double business bound,
I stand in pause where I shall first begin,
And both neglect. What if this cursed hand
Were thicker than itself with brother's blood,
Is there not rain enough in the sweet heavens
To wash it white as snow? Whereto serves mercy

But to confront the visage of offence?
And what's in prayer but this two-fold force,
To be forestalled ere we come to fall,
Or pardon'd being down? Then I'll look up;
My fault is past. But, O, what form of prayer
Can serve my turn? 'Forgive me my foul murder'?
That cannot be; since I am still possess'd
Of those effects for which I did the murder,
My crown, mine own ambition and my queen.
May one be pardon'd and retain the offence?
In the corrupted currents of this world
Offence's gilded hand may shove by justice,
And oft 'tis seen the wicked prize itself
Buys out the law: but 'tis not so above;
There is no shuffling, there the action lies
In his true nature; and we ourselves compell'd,
Even to the teeth and forehead of our faults,
To give in evidence. What then? what rests?
Try what repentance can: what can it not?
Yet what can it when one can not repent?
O wretched state! O bosom black as death!
O limed soul, that, struggling to be free,
Art more engaged! Help, angels! Make assay!
Bow, stubborn knees; and, heart with strings of steel,
Be soft as sinews of the newborn babe!
All may be well.

Retires and kneels

Enter HAMLET

HAMLET
Now might I do it pat, now he is praying;
And now I'll do't. And so he goes to heaven;

And so am I revenged. That would be scann'd:
A villain kills my father; and for that,
I, his sole son, do this same villain send
To heaven.
O, this is hire and salary, not revenge.
He took my father grossly, full of bread;
With all his crimes broad blown, as flush as May;
And how his audit stands who knows save heaven?
But in our circumstance and course of thought,
'Tis heavy with him: and am I then revenged,
To take him in the purging of his soul,
When he is fit and season'd for his passage?
No!
Up, sword; and know thou a more horrid hent:
When he is drunk asleep, or in his rage,
Or in the incestuous pleasure of his bed;
At gaming, swearing, or about some act
That has no relish of salvation in't;
Then trip him, that his heels may kick at heaven,
And that his soul may be as damn'd and black
As hell, whereto it goes. My mother stays:
This physic but prolongs thy sickly days.

Exit

KING CLAUDIUS
[Rising] My words fly up, my thoughts remain below:
Words without thoughts never to heaven go.

Exit

SCENE IV.

The Queen's closet.

Enter QUEEN GERTRUDE and POLONIUS

LORD POLONIUS
>He will come straight. Look you lay home to him:
>Tell him his pranks have been too broad to bear with,
>And that your grace hath screen'd and stood between
>Much heat and him. I'll sconce me even here.
>Pray you, be round with him.

HAMLET
>[Within] Mother, mother, mother!

QUEEN GERTRUDE
>I'll warrant you,
>Fear me not: withdraw, I hear him coming.

POLONIUS hides behind the arras

Enter HAMLET

HAMLET
>Now, mother, what's the matter?

QUEEN GERTRUDE
>Hamlet, thou hast thy father much offended.

HAMLET
>Mother, you have my father much offended.

QUEEN GERTRUDE
>Come, come, you answer with an idle tongue.

HAMLET
>Go, go, you question with a wicked tongue.

QUEEN GERTRUDE
>Why, how now, Hamlet!

HAMLET
>What's the matter now?

QUEEN GERTRUDE
  Have you forgot me?
HAMLET
  No, by the rood, not so:
  You are the queen, your husband's brother's wife;
  And--would it were not so!--you are my mother.
QUEEN GERTRUDE
  Nay, then, I'll set those to you that can speak.
HAMLET
  Come, come, and sit you down; you shall not budge;
  You go not till I set you up a glass
  Where you may see the inmost part of you.
QUEEN GERTRUDE
  What wilt thou do? thou wilt not murder me?
  Help, help, ho!
LORD POLONIUS
  [Behind] What, ho! help, help, help!
HAMLET
  [Drawing] How now! a rat? Dead, for a ducat, dead!

Makes a pass through the arras

LORD POLONIUS
  [Behind] O, I am slain!

Falls and dies

QUEEN GERTRUDE
  O me, what hast thou done?
HAMLET
  Nay, I know not:
  Is it the king?
QUEEN GERTRUDE
  O, what a rash and bloody deed is this!
HAMLET

A bloody deed! almost as bad, good mother,
As kill a king, and marry with his brother.
QUEEN GERTRUDE
 As kill a king!
HAMLET
 Ay, lady, 'twas my word.

   Lifts up the array and discovers POLONIUS

Thou wretched, rash, intruding fool, farewell!
I took thee for thy better: take thy fortune;
Thou find'st to be too busy is some danger.
Leave wringing of your hands: peace! sit you down,
And let me wring your heart; for so I shall,
If it be made of penetrable stuff,
If damned custom have not brass'd it so
That it is proof and bulwark against sense.
QUEEN GERTRUDE
 What have I done, that thou darest wag thy tongue
 In noise so rude against me?
HAMLET
 Such an act
 That blurs the grace and blush of modesty,
 Calls virtue hypocrite, takes off the rose
 From the fair forehead of an innocent love
 And sets a blister there, makes marriage-vows
 As false as dicers' oaths: O, such a deed
 As from the body of contraction plucks
 The very soul, and sweet religion makes
 A rhapsody of words: heaven's face doth glow:
 Yea, this solidity and compound mass,
 With tristful visage, as against the doom,
 Is thought-sick at the act.
QUEEN GERTRUDE
 Ay me, what act,

That roars so loud, and thunders in the index?
HAMLET
Look here, upon this picture, and on this,
The counterfeit presentment of two brothers.
See, what a grace was seated on this brow;
Hyperion's curls; the front of Jove himself;
An eye like Mars, to threaten and command;
A station like the herald Mercury
New-lighted on a heaven-kissing hill;
A combination and a form indeed,
Where every god did seem to set his seal,
To give the world assurance of a man:
This was your husband. Look you now, what follows:
Here is your husband; like a mildew'd ear,
Blasting his wholesome brother. Have you eyes?
Could you on this fair mountain leave to feed,
And batten on this moor? Ha! have you eyes?
You cannot call it love; for at your age
The hey-day in the blood is tame, it's humble,
And waits upon the judgment: and what judgment
Would step from this to this? Sense, sure, you have,
Else could you not have motion; but sure, that sense
Is apoplex'd; for madness would not err,
Nor sense to ecstasy was ne'er so thrall'd
But it reserved some quantity of choice,
To serve in such a difference. What devil was't
That thus hath cozen'd you at hoodman-blind?
Eyes without feeling, feeling without sight,
Ears without hands or eyes, smelling sans all,
Or but a sickly part of one true sense
Could not so mope.
O shame! where is thy blush? Rebellious hell,
If thou canst mutine in a matron's bones,
To flaming youth let virtue be as wax,

And melt in her own fire: proclaim no shame
When the compulsive ardour gives the charge,
Since frost itself as actively doth burn
And reason panders will.

QUEEN GERTRUDE

O Hamlet, speak no more:
Thou turn'st mine eyes into my very soul;
And there I see such black and grained spots
As will not leave their tinct.

HAMLET

Nay, but to live
In the rank sweat of an enseamed bed,
Stew'd in corruption, honeying and making love
Over the nasty sty,--

QUEEN GERTRUDE

O, speak to me no more;
These words, like daggers, enter in mine ears;
No more, sweet Hamlet!

HAMLET

A murderer and a villain;
A slave that is not twentieth part the tithe
Of your precedent lord; a vice of kings;
A cutpurse of the empire and the rule,
That from a shelf the precious diadem stole,
And put it in his pocket!

QUEEN GERTRUDE

No more!

HAMLET

A king of shreds and patches,--

Enter Ghost

Save me, and hover o'er me with your wings,
You heavenly guards! What would your gracious figure?

QUEEN GERTRUDE

Alas, he's mad!
HAMLET
Do you not come your tardy son to chide,
That, lapsed in time and passion, lets go by
The important acting of your dread command? O, say!
Ghost
Do not forget: this visitation
Is but to whet thy almost blunted purpose.
But, look, amazement on thy mother sits:
O, step between her and her fighting soul:
Conceit in weakest bodies strongest works:
Speak to her, Hamlet.
HAMLET
How is it with you, lady?
QUEEN GERTRUDE
Alas, how is't with you,
That you do bend your eye on vacancy
And with the incorporal air do hold discourse?
Forth at your eyes your spirits wildly peep;
And, as the sleeping soldiers in the alarm,
Your bedded hair, like life in excrements,
Starts up, and stands on end. O gentle son,
Upon the heat and flame of thy distemper
Sprinkle cool patience. Whereon do you look?
HAMLET
On him, on him! Look you, how pale he glares!
His form and cause conjoin'd, preaching to stones,
Would make them capable. Do not look upon me;
Lest with this piteous action you convert
My stern effects: then what I have to do
Will want true colour; tears perchance for blood.
QUEEN GERTRUDE
To whom do you speak this?
HAMLET

Do you see nothing there?
QUEEN GERTRUDE
  Nothing at all; yet all that is I see.
HAMLET
  Nor did you nothing hear?
QUEEN GERTRUDE
  No, nothing but ourselves.
HAMLET
  Why, look you there! look, how it steals away!
  My father, in his habit as he lived!
  Look, where he goes, even now, out at the portal!

Exit Ghost

QUEEN GERTRUDE
  This the very coinage of your brain:
  This bodiless creation ecstasy
  Is very cunning in.
HAMLET
  Ecstasy!
  My pulse, as yours, doth temperately keep time,
  And makes as healthful music: it is not madness
  That I have utter'd: bring me to the test,
  And I the matter will re-word; which madness
  Would gambol from. Mother, for love of grace,
  Lay not that mattering unction to your soul,
  That not your trespass, but my madness speaks:
  It will but skin and film the ulcerous place,
  Whilst rank corruption, mining all within,
  Infects unseen. Confess yourself to heaven;
  Repent what's past; avoid what is to come;
  And do not spread the compost on the weeds,
  To make them ranker. Forgive me this my virtue;
  For in the fatness of these pursy times
  Virtue itself of vice must pardon beg,

Yea, curb and woo for leave to do him good.
QUEEN GERTRUDE
O Hamlet, thou hast cleft my heart in twain.
HAMLET
O, throw away the worser part of it,
And live the purer with the other half.
Good night: but go not to mine uncle's bed;
Assume a virtue, if you have it not.
That monster, custom, who all sense doth eat,
Of habits devil, is angel yet in this,
That to the use of actions fair and good
He likewise gives a frock or livery,
That aptly is put on. Refrain to-night,
And that shall lend a kind of easiness
To the next abstinence: the next more easy;
For use almost can change the stamp of nature,
And either [ ] the devil, or throw him out
With wondrous potency. Once more, good night:
And when you are desirous to be bless'd,
I'll blessing beg of you. For this same lord,

Pointing to POLONIUS

I do repent: but heaven hath pleased it so,
To punish me with this and this with me,
That I must be their scourge and minister.
I will bestow him, and will answer well
The death I gave him. So, again, good night.
I must be cruel, only to be kind:
Thus bad begins and worse remains behind.
One word more, good lady.
QUEEN GERTRUDE
What shall I do?
HAMLET
Not this, by no means, that I bid you do:

Let the bloat king tempt you again to bed;
Pinch wanton on your cheek; call you his mouse;
And let him, for a pair of reechy kisses,
Or paddling in your neck with his damn'd fingers,
Make you to ravel all this matter out,
That I essentially am not in madness,
But mad in craft. 'Twere good you let him know;
For who, that's but a queen, fair, sober, wise,
Would from a paddock, from a bat, a gib,
Such dear concernings hide? who would do so?
No, in despite of sense and secrecy,
Unpeg the basket on the house's top.
Let the birds fly, and, like the famous ape,
To try conclusions, in the basket creep,
And break your own neck down.

QUEEN GERTRUDE

Be thou assured, if words be made of breath,
And breath of life, I have no life to breathe
What thou hast said to me.

HAMLET

I must to England; you know that?

QUEEN GERTRUDE

Alack,
I had forgot: 'tis so concluded on.

HAMLET

There's letters seal'd: and my two schoolfellows,
Whom I will trust as I will adders fang'd,
They bear the mandate; they must sweep my way,
And marshal me to knavery. Let it work;
For 'tis the sport to have the engineer
Hoist with his own petard: and 't shall go hard
But I will delve one yard below their mines,
And blow them at the moon: O, 'tis most sweet,
When in one line two crafts directly meet.

This man shall set me packing:
I'll lug the guts into the neighbour room.
Mother, good night. Indeed this counsellor
Is now most still, most secret and most grave,
Who was in life a foolish prating knave.
Come, sir, to draw toward an end with you.
Good night, mother.

Exeunt severally; HAMLET dragging in POLONIUS

ACT IV

SCENE I.

A room in the castle.

*Enter KING CLAUDIUS, QUEEN GERTRUDE,
ROSENCRANTZ, and GUILDENSTERN*

KING CLAUDIUS
    There's matter in these sighs, these profound heaves:
    You must translate: 'tis fit we understand them.
    Where is your son?
QUEEN GERTRUDE
    Bestow this place on us a little while.

Exeunt ROSENCRANTZ and GUILDENSTERN

    Ah, my good lord, what have I seen to-night!
KING CLAUDIUS
    What, Gertrude? How does Hamlet?
QUEEN GERTRUDE
    Mad as the sea and wind, when both contend
    Which is the mightier: in his lawless fit,
    Behind the arras hearing something stir,
    Whips out his rapier, cries, 'A rat, a rat!'
    And, in this brainish apprehension, kills
    The unseen good old man.
KING CLAUDIUS
    O heavy deed!
    It had been so with us, had we been there:
    His liberty is full of threats to all;
    To you yourself, to us, to every one.
    Alas, how shall this bloody deed be answer'd?
    It will be laid to us, whose providence

Should have kept short, restrain'd and out of haunt,
This mad young man: but so much was our love,
We would not understand what was most fit;
But, like the owner of a foul disease,
To keep it from divulging, let it feed
Even on the pith of Life. Where is he gone?

QUEEN GERTRUDE

To draw apart the body he hath kill'd:
O'er whom his very madness, like some ore
Among a mineral of metals base,
Shows itself pure; he weeps for what is done.

KING CLAUDIUS

O Gertrude, come away!
The sun no sooner shall the mountains touch,
But we will ship him hence: and this vile deed
We must, with all our majesty and skill,
Both countenance and excuse. Ho, Guildenstern!

Re-enter ROSENCRANTZ and GUILDENSTERN

Friends both, go join you with some further aid:
Hamlet in madness hath Polonius slain,
And from his mother's closet hath he dragg'd him:
Go seek him out; speak fair, and bring the body
Into the chapel. I pray you, haste in this.

Exeunt ROSENCRANTZ and GUILDENSTERN

Come, Gertrude, we'll call up our wisest friends;
And let them know, both what we mean to do,
And what's untimely done. O, come away!
My soul is full of discord and dismay.

Exeunt

SCENE II.

Another room in the castle.

Enter HAMLET

HAMLET

Safely stowed.

ROSENCRANTZ: GUILDENSTERN:

[Within] Hamlet! Lord Hamlet!

HAMLET

What noise? who calls on Hamlet?

O, here they come.

Enter ROSENCRANTZ and GUILDENSTERN

ROSENCRANTZ

What have you done, my lord, with the dead body?

HAMLET

Compounded it with dust, whereto 'tis kin.

ROSENCRANTZ

Tell us where 'tis, that we may take it thence

And bear it to the chapel.

HAMLET

Do not believe it.

ROSENCRANTZ

Believe what?

HAMLET

That I can keep your counsel and not mine own.

Besides, to be demanded of a sponge! what

replication should be made by the son of a king?

ROSENCRANTZ

Take you me for a sponge, my lord?

HAMLET

Ay, sir, that soaks up the king's countenance, his

rewards, his authorities. But such officers do the

king best service in the end: he keeps them, like

an ape, in the corner of his jaw; first mouthed, to
be last swallowed: when he needs what you have
gleaned, it is but squeezing you, and, sponge, you
shall be dry again.

ROSENCRANTZ

I understand you not, my lord.

HAMLET

I am glad of it: a knavish speech sleeps in a
foolish ear.

ROSENCRANTZ

My lord, you must tell us where the body is, and go
with us to the king.

HAMLET

The body is with the king, but the king is not with
the body. The king is a thing--

GUILDENSTERN

A thing, my lord!

HAMLET

Of nothing: bring me to him. Hide fox, and all after.

Exeunt

SCENE III.

Another room in the castle.

Enter KING CLAUDIUS, attended

KING CLAUDIUS

I have sent to seek him, and to find the body.
How dangerous is it that this man goes loose!
Yet must not we put the strong law on him:
He's loved of the distracted multitude,
Who like not in their judgment, but their eyes;
And where tis so, the offender's scourge is weigh'd,
But never the offence. To bear all smooth and even,

This sudden sending him away must seem
Deliberate pause: diseases desperate grown
By desperate appliance are relieved,
Or not at all.

Enter ROSENCRANTZ

How now! what hath befall'n?
ROSENCRANTZ
Where the dead body is bestow'd, my lord,
We cannot get from him.
KING CLAUDIUS
But where is he?
ROSENCRANTZ
Without, my lord; guarded, to know your pleasure.
KING CLAUDIUS
Bring him before us.
ROSENCRANTZ
Ho, Guildenstern! bring in my lord.

Enter HAMLET and GUILDENSTERN

KING CLAUDIUS
Now, Hamlet, where's Polonius?
HAMLET
At supper.
KING CLAUDIUS
At supper! where?
HAMLET
Not where he eats, but where he is eaten: a certain
convocation of politic worms are e'en at him. Your
worm is your only emperor for diet: we fat all
creatures else to fat us, and we fat ourselves for
maggots: your fat king and your lean beggar is but
variable service, two dishes, but to one table:

that's the end.

KING CLAUDIUS

Alas, alas!

HAMLET

A man may fish with the worm that hath eat of a
king, and eat of the fish that hath fed of that worm.

KING CLAUDIUS

What dost you mean by this?

HAMLET

Nothing but to show you how a king may go a
progress through the guts of a beggar.

KING CLAUDIUS

Where is Polonius?

HAMLET

In heaven; send hither to see: if your messenger
find him not there, seek him i' the other place
yourself. But indeed, if you find him not within
this month, you shall nose him as you go up the
stairs into the lobby.

KING CLAUDIUS

Go seek him there.

To some Attendants

HAMLET

He will stay till ye come.

Exeunt Attendants

KING CLAUDIUS

Hamlet, this deed, for thine especial safety,--
Which we do tender, as we dearly grieve
For that which thou hast done,--must send thee hence
With fiery quickness: therefore prepare thyself;
The bark is ready, and the wind at help,

The associates tend, and every thing is bent
For England.
KING CLAUDIUS

HAMLET
For England!
KING CLAUDIUS
Ay, Hamlet.
HAMLET
Good.
KING CLAUDIUS
So is it, if thou knew'st our purposes.
HAMLET
I see a cherub that sees them. But, come; for
England! Farewell, dear mother.
KING CLAUDIUS
Thy loving father, Hamlet.
HAMLET
My mother: father and mother is man and wife; man
and wife is one flesh; and so, my mother. Come, for
England!

Exit

KING CLAUDIUS
Follow him at foot; tempt him with speed aboard;
Delay it not; I'll have him hence to-night:
Away! for every thing is seal'd and done
That else leans on the affair: pray you, make haste.

Exeunt ROSENCRANTZ and GUILDENSTERN

And, England, if my love thou hold'st at aught--
As my great power thereof may give thee sense,
Since yet thy cicatrice looks raw and red
After the Danish sword, and thy free awe
Pays homage to us--thou mayst not coldly set

Our sovereign process; which imports at full,
By letters congruing to that effect,
The present death of Hamlet. Do it, England;
For like the hectic in my blood he rages,
And thou must cure me: till I know 'tis done,
Howe'er my haps, my joys were ne'er begun.

Exit

SCENE IV.

A plain in Denmark.

Enter FORTINBRAS, a Captain, and Soldiers, marching

PRINCE FORTINBRAS
Go, captain, from me greet the Danish king;
Tell him that, by his licence, Fortinbras
Craves the conveyance of a promised march
Over his kingdom. You know the rendezvous.
If that his majesty would aught with us,
We shall express our duty in his eye;
And let him know so.
Captain
I will do't, my lord.
PRINCE FORTINBRAS
Go softly on.

Exeunt FORTINBRAS and Soldiers

*Enter HAMLET, ROSENCRANTZ, GUILDENSTERN, and
others*

HAMLET
Good sir, whose powers are these?
Captain

They are of Norway, sir.
HAMLET
How purposed, sir, I pray you?
Captain
Against some part of Poland.
HAMLET
Who commands them, sir?
Captain
The nephews to old Norway, Fortinbras.
HAMLET
Goes it against the main of Poland, sir,
Or for some frontier?
Captain
Truly to speak, and with no addition,
We go to gain a little patch of ground
That hath in it no profit but the name.
To pay five ducats, five, I would not farm it;
Nor will it yield to Norway or the Pole
A ranker rate, should it be sold in fee.
HAMLET
Why, then the Polack never will defend it.
Captain
Yes, it is already garrison'd.
HAMLET
Two thousand souls and twenty thousand ducats
Will not debate the question of this straw:
This is the imposthume of much wealth and peace,
That inward breaks, and shows no cause without
Why the man dies. I humbly thank you, sir.
Captain
God be wi' you, sir.

Exit

ROSENCRANTZ

Wilt please you go, my lord?
HAMLET
I'll be with you straight go a little before.

Exeunt all except HAMLET

How all occasions do inform against me,
And spur my dull revenge! What is a man,
If his chief good and market of his time
Be but to sleep and feed? a beast, no more.
Sure, he that made us with such large discourse,
Looking before and after, gave us not
That capability and god-like reason
To fust in us unused. Now, whether it be
Bestial oblivion, or some craven scruple
Of thinking too precisely on the event,
A thought which, quarter'd, hath but one part wisdom
And ever three parts coward, I do not know
Why yet I live to say 'This thing's to do;'
Sith I have cause and will and strength and means
To do't. Examples gross as earth exhort me:
Witness this army of such mass and charge
Led by a delicate and tender prince,
Whose spirit with divine ambition puff'd
Makes mouths at the invisible event,
Exposing what is mortal and unsure
To all that fortune, death and danger dare,
Even for an egg-shell. Rightly to be great
Is not to stir without great argument,
But greatly to find quarrel in a straw
When honour's at the stake. How stand I then,
That have a father kill'd, a mother stain'd,
Excitements of my reason and my blood,
And let all sleep? while, to my shame, I see
The imminent death of twenty thousand men,

That, for a fantasy and trick of fame,
Go to their graves like beds, fight for a plot
Whereon the numbers cannot try the cause,
Which is not tomb enough and continent
To hide the slain? O, from this time forth,
My thoughts be bloody, or be nothing worth!

Exit

SCENE V.

Elsinore. A room in the castle.

Enter QUEEN GERTRUDE, HORATIO, and a Gentleman

QUEEN GERTRUDE
  I will not speak with her.
Gentleman
  She is importunate, indeed distract:
  Her mood will needs be pitied.
QUEEN GERTRUDE
  What would she have?
Gentleman
  She speaks much of her father; says she hears
  There's tricks i' the world; and hems, and beats her
  heart;
  Spurns enviously at straws; speaks things in doubt,
  That carry but half sense: her speech is nothing,
  Yet the unshaped use of it doth move
  The hearers to collection; they aim at it,
  And botch the words up fit to their own thoughts;
  Which, as her winks, and nods, and gestures
  yield them,
  Indeed would make one think there might be thought,
  Though nothing sure, yet much unhappily.
HORATIO

'Twere good she were spoken with; for she may strew
Dangerous conjectures in ill-breeding minds.
QUEEN GERTRUDE
Let her come in.

Exit HORATIO

To my sick soul, as sin's true nature is,
Each toy seems prologue to some great amiss:
So full of artless jealousy is guilt,
It spills itself in fearing to be spilt.

Re-enter HORATIO, with OPHELIA

OPHELIA
Where is the beauteous majesty of Denmark?
QUEEN GERTRUDE
How now, Ophelia!
OPHELIA
[Sings]
How should I your true love know
From another one?
By his cockle hat and staff,
And his sandal shoon.
QUEEN GERTRUDE
Alas, sweet lady, what imports this song?
OPHELIA
Say you? nay, pray you, mark.

Sings

He is dead and gone, lady,
He is dead and gone;
At his head a grass-green turf,
At his heels a stone.
QUEEN GERTRUDE

Nay, but, Ophelia,--
OPHELIA
Pray you, mark.

Sings

White his shroud as the mountain snow,--

Enter KING CLAUDIUS

QUEEN GERTRUDE
Alas, look here, my lord.
OPHELIA
[Sings]
Larded with sweet flowers
Which bewept to the grave did go
With true-love showers.
KING CLAUDIUS
How do you, pretty lady?
OPHELIA
Well, God 'ild you! They say the owl was a baker's
daughter. Lord, we know what we are, but know not
what we may be. God be at your table!
KING CLAUDIUS
Conceit upon her father.
OPHELIA
Pray you, let's have no words of this; but when they
ask you what it means, say you this:

Sings

To-morrow is Saint Valentine's day,
All in the morning betime,
And I a maid at your window,
To be your Valentine.
Then up he rose, and donn'd his clothes,

And dupp'd the chamber-door;
Let in the maid, that out a maid
Never departed more.

KING CLAUDIUS

Pretty Ophelia!

OPHELIA

Indeed, la, without an oath, I'll make an end on't:

Sings

By Gis and by Saint Charity,
Alack, and fie for shame!
Young men will do't, if they come to't;
By cock, they are to blame.
Quoth she, before you tumbled me,
You promised me to wed.
So would I ha' done, by yonder sun,
An thou hadst not come to my bed.

KING CLAUDIUS

How long hath she been thus?

OPHELIA

I hope all will be well. We must be patient: but I
cannot choose but weep, to think they should lay him
i' the cold ground. My brother shall know of it:
and so I thank you for your good counsel. Come, my
coach! Good night, ladies; good night, sweet ladies;
good night, good night.

Exit

KING CLAUDIUS

Follow her close; give her good watch,
I pray you.

Exit HORATIO

O, this is the poison of deep grief; it springs
All from her father's death. O Gertrude, Gertrude,
When sorrows come, they come not single spies
But in battalions. First, her father slain:
Next, your son gone; and he most violent author
Of his own just remove: the people muddied,
Thick and unwholesome in their thoughts and whispers,
For good Polonius' death; and we have done but greenly,
In hugger-mugger to inter him: poor Ophelia
Divided from herself and her fair judgment,
Without the which we are pictures, or mere beasts:
Last, and as much containing as all these,
Her brother is in secret come from France;
Feeds on his wonder, keeps himself in clouds,
And wants not buzzers to infect his ear
With pestilent speeches of his father's death;
Wherein necessity, of matter beggar'd,
Will nothing stick our person to arraign
In ear and ear. O my dear Gertrude, this,
Like to a murdering-piece, in many places
Gives me superfluous death.

A noise within

QUEEN GERTRUDE
   Alack, what noise is this?
KING CLAUDIUS
   Where are my Switzers? Let them guard the door.

Enter another Gentleman

   What is the matter?
Gentleman
   Save yourself, my lord:
   The ocean, overpeering of his list,

Eats not the flats with more impetuous haste
Than young Laertes, in a riotous head,
O'erbears your officers. The rabble call him lord;
And, as the world were now but to begin,
Antiquity forgot, custom not known,
The ratifiers and props of every word,
They cry 'Choose we: Laertes shall be king:'
Caps, hands, and tongues, applaud it to the clouds:
'Laertes shall be king, Laertes king!'

QUEEN GERTRUDE
How cheerfully on the false trail they cry!
O, this is counter, you false Danish dogs!

KING CLAUDIUS
The doors are broke.

Noise within

Enter LAERTES, armed; Danes following

LAERTES
Where is this king? Sirs, stand you all without.

Danes
No, let's come in.

LAERTES
I pray you, give me leave.

Danes
We will, we will.

They retire without the door

LAERTES
I thank you: keep the door. O thou vile king,
Give me my father!

QUEEN GERTRUDE
Calmly, good Laertes.

LAERTES
    That drop of blood that's calm proclaims me bastard,
    Cries cuckold to my father, brands the harlot
    Even here, between the chaste unsmirched brow
    Of my true mother.
KING CLAUDIUS
    What is the cause, Laertes,
    That thy rebellion looks so giant-like?
    Let him go, Gertrude; do not fear our person:
    There's such divinity doth hedge a king,
    That treason can but peep to what it would,
    Acts little of his will. Tell me, Laertes,
    Why thou art thus incensed. Let him go, Gertrude.
    Speak, man.
LAERTES
    Where is my father?
KING CLAUDIUS
    Dead.
QUEEN GERTRUDE
    But not by him.
KING CLAUDIUS
    Let him demand his fill.
LAERTES
    How came he dead? I'll not be juggled with:
    To hell, allegiance! vows, to the blackest devil!
    Conscience and grace, to the profoundest pit!
    I dare damnation. To this point I stand,
    That both the worlds I give to negligence,
    Let come what comes; only I'll be revenged
    Most thoroughly for my father.
KING CLAUDIUS
    Who shall stay you?
LAERTES
    My will, not all the world:

And for my means, I'll husband them so well,
They shall go far with little.
KING CLAUDIUS
Good Laertes,
If you desire to know the certainty
Of your dear father's death, is't writ in your revenge,
That, swoopstake, you will draw both friend and foe,
Winner and loser?
LAERTES
None but his enemies.
KING CLAUDIUS
Will you know them then?
LAERTES
To his good friends thus wide I'll ope my arms;
And like the kind life-rendering pelican,
Repast them with my blood.
KING CLAUDIUS
Why, now you speak
Like a good child and a true gentleman.
That I am guiltless of your father's death,
And am most sensible in grief for it,
It shall as level to your judgment pierce
As day does to your eye.
Danes
[Within] Let her come in.
LAERTES
How now! what noise is that?

Re-enter OPHELIA

O heat, dry up my brains! tears seven times salt,
Burn out the sense and virtue of mine eye!
By heaven, thy madness shall be paid by weight,
Till our scale turn the beam. O rose of May!
Dear maid, kind sister, sweet Ophelia!

O heavens! is't possible, a young maid's wits
Should be as moral as an old man's life?
Nature is fine in love, and where 'tis fine,
It sends some precious instance of itself
After the thing it loves.

OPHELIA

[Sings]
They bore him barefaced on the bier;
Hey non nonny, nonny, hey nonny;
And in his grave rain'd many a tear:--
Fare you well, my dove!

LAERTES

Hadst thou thy wits, and didst persuade revenge,
It could not move thus.

OPHELIA

[Sings]
You must sing a-down a-down,
An you call him a-down-a.
O, how the wheel becomes it! It is the false
steward, that stole his master's daughter.

LAERTES

This nothing's more than matter.

OPHELIA

There's rosemary, that's for remembrance; pray,
love, remember: and there is pansies. that's for thoughts.

LAERTES

A document in madness, thoughts and remembrance
fitted.

OPHELIA

There's fennel for you, and columbines: there's rue
for you; and here's some for me: we may call it
herb-grace o' Sundays: O you must wear your rue with
a difference. There's a daisy: I would give you
some violets, but they withered all when my father

died: they say he made a good end,--

Sings

For bonny sweet Robin is all my joy.
LAERTES
Thought and affliction, passion, hell itself,
She turns to favour and to prettiness.
OPHELIA
[Sings]
And will he not come again?
And will he not come again?
No, no, he is dead:
Go to thy death-bed:
He never will come again.
His beard was as white as snow,
All flaxen was his poll:
He is gone, he is gone,
And we cast away moan:
God ha' mercy on his soul!
And of all Christian souls, I pray God. God be wi' ye.

Exit

LAERTES
Do you see this, O God?
KING CLAUDIUS
Laertes, I must commune with your grief,
Or you deny me right. Go but apart,
Make choice of whom your wisest friends you will.
And they shall hear and judge 'twixt you and me:
If by direct or by collateral hand
They find us touch'd, we will our kingdom give,
Our crown, our life, and all that we can ours,
To you in satisfaction; but if not,

Be you content to lend your patience to us,
And we shall jointly labour with your soul
To give it due content.

LAERTES

Let this be so;
His means of death, his obscure funeral--
No trophy, sword, nor hatchment o'er his bones,
No noble rite nor formal ostentation--
Cry to be heard, as 'twere from heaven to earth,
That I must call't in question.

KING CLAUDIUS

So you shall;
And where the offence is let the great axe fall.
I pray you, go with me.

Exeunt

SCENE VI.

Another room in the castle.

Enter HORATIO and a Servant

HORATIO

What are they that would speak with me?

Servant

Sailors, sir: they say they have letters for you.

HORATIO

Let them come in.

Exit Servant

I do not know from what part of the world
I should be greeted, if not from Lord Hamlet.

Enter Sailors

First Sailor

God bless you, sir.

HORATIO

Let him bless thee too.

First Sailor

He shall, sir, an't please him. There's a letter for
you, sir; it comes from the ambassador that was
bound for England; if your name be Horatio, as I am
let to know it is.

HORATIO

[Reads] 'Horatio, when thou shalt have overlooked
this, give these fellows some means to the king:
they have letters for him. Ere we were two days old
at sea, a pirate of very warlike appointment gave us
chase. Finding ourselves too slow of sail, we put on
a compelled valour, and in the grapple I boarded
them: on the instant they got clear of our ship; so
I alone became their prisoner. They have dealt with
me like thieves of mercy: but they knew what they
did; I am to do a good turn for them. Let the king
have the letters I have sent; and repair thou to me
with as much speed as thou wouldst fly death. I
have words to speak in thine ear will make thee
dumb; yet are they much too light for the bore of
the matter. These good fellows will bring thee
where I am. Rosencrantz and Guildenstern hold their
course for England: of them I have much to tell
thee. Farewell.

'He that thou knowest thine, HAMLET.'

Come, I will make you way for these your letters;
And do't the speedier, that you may direct me
To him from whom you brought them.

Exeunt

SCENE VII.

Another room in the castle.

Enter KING CLAUDIUS and LAERTES

KING CLAUDIUS

 Now must your conscience my acquaintance seal,
 And you must put me in your heart for friend,
 Sith you have heard, and with a knowing ear,
 That he which hath your noble father slain
 Pursued my life.

LAERTES

 It well appears: but tell me
 Why you proceeded not against these feats,
 So crimeful and so capital in nature,
 As by your safety, wisdom, all things else,
 You mainly were stirr'd up.

KING CLAUDIUS

 O, for two special reasons;
 Which may to you, perhaps, seem much unsinew'd,
 But yet to me they are strong. The queen his mother
 Lives almost by his looks; and for myself--
 My virtue or my plague, be it either which--
 She's so conjunctive to my life and soul,
 That, as the star moves not but in his sphere,
 I could not but by her. The other motive,
 Why to a public count I might not go,
 Is the great love the general gender bear him;
 Who, dipping all his faults in their affection,
 Would, like the spring that turneth wood to stone,
 Convert his gyves to graces; so that my arrows,
 Too slightly timber'd for so loud a wind,
 Would have reverted to my bow again,
 And not where I had aim'd them.

LAERTES

And so have I a noble father lost;
A sister driven into desperate terms,
Whose worth, if praises may go back again,
Stood challenger on mount of all the age
For her perfections: but my revenge will come.
KING CLAUDIUS
Break not your sleeps for that: you must not think
That we are made of stuff so flat and dull
That we can let our beard be shook with danger
And think it pastime. You shortly shall hear more:
I loved your father, and we love ourself;
And that, I hope, will teach you to imagine--

Enter a Messenger

How now! what news?
Messenger
Letters, my lord, from Hamlet:
This to your majesty; this to the queen.
KING CLAUDIUS
From Hamlet! who brought them?
Messenger
Sailors, my lord, they say; I saw them not:
They were given me by Claudio; he received them
Of him that brought them.
KING CLAUDIUS
Laertes, you shall hear them. Leave us.

Exit Messenger

Reads

'High and mighty, You shall know I am set naked on
your kingdom. To-morrow shall I beg leave to see
your kingly eyes: when I shall, first asking your

pardon thereunto, recount the occasion of my sudden
and more strange return. 'HAMLET.'
What should this mean? Are all the rest come back?
Or is it some abuse, and no such thing?
LAERTES
 Know you the hand?
KING CLAUDIUS
 'Tis Hamlets character. 'Naked!
 And in a postscript here, he says 'alone.'
 Can you advise me?
LAERTES
 I'm lost in it, my lord. But let him come;
 It warms the very sickness in my heart,
 That I shall live and tell him to his teeth,
 'Thus didest thou.'
KING CLAUDIUS
 If it be so, Laertes--
 As how should it be so? how otherwise?--
 Will you be ruled by me?
LAERTES
 Ay, my lord;
 So you will not o'errule me to a peace.
KING CLAUDIUS
 To thine own peace. If he be now return'd,
 As checking at his voyage, and that he means
 No more to undertake it, I will work him
 To an exploit, now ripe in my device,
 Under the which he shall not choose but fall:
 And for his death no wind of blame shall breathe,
 But even his mother shall uncharge the practise
 And call it accident.
LAERTES
 My lord, I will be ruled;
 The rather, if you could devise it so

That I might be the organ.
KING CLAUDIUS
    It falls right.
    You have been talk'd of since your travel much,
    And that in Hamlet's hearing, for a quality
    Wherein, they say, you shine: your sum of parts
    Did not together pluck such envy from him
    As did that one, and that, in my regard,
    Of the unworthiest siege.
LAERTES
    What part is that, my lord?
KING CLAUDIUS
    A very riband in the cap of youth,
    Yet needful too; for youth no less becomes
    The light and careless livery that it wears
    Than settled age his sables and his weeds,
    Importing health and graveness. Two months since,
    Here was a gentleman of Normandy:--
    I've seen myself, and served against, the French,
    And they can well on horseback: but this gallant
    Had witchcraft in't; he grew unto his seat;
    And to such wondrous doing brought his horse,
    As he had been incorpsed and demi-natured
    With the brave beast: so far he topp'd my thought,
    That I, in forgery of shapes and tricks,
    Come short of what he did.
LAERTES
    A Norman was't?
KING CLAUDIUS
    A Norman.
LAERTES
    Upon my life, Lamond.
KING CLAUDIUS
    The very same.

LAERTES

I know him well: he is the brooch indeed
And gem of all the nation.

KING CLAUDIUS

He made confession of you,
And gave you such a masterly report
For art and exercise in your defence
And for your rapier most especially,
That he cried out, 'twould be a sight indeed,
If one could match you: the scrimers of their nation,
He swore, had had neither motion, guard, nor eye,
If you opposed them. Sir, this report of his
Did Hamlet so envenom with his envy
That he could nothing do but wish and beg
Your sudden coming o'er, to play with him.
Now, out of this,--

LAERTES

What out of this, my lord?

KING CLAUDIUS

Laertes, was your father dear to you?
Or are you like the painting of a sorrow,
A face without a heart?

LAERTES

Why ask you this?

KING CLAUDIUS

Not that I think you did not love your father;
But that I know love is begun by time;
And that I see, in passages of proof,
Time qualifies the spark and fire of it.
There lives within the very flame of love
A kind of wick or snuff that will abate it;
And nothing is at a like goodness still;
For goodness, growing to a plurisy,
Dies in his own too much: that we would do

We should do when we would; for this 'would' changes
And hath abatements and delays as many
As there are tongues, are hands, are accidents;
And then this 'should' is like a spendthrift sigh,
That hurts by easing. But, to the quick o' the ulcer:--
Hamlet comes back: what would you undertake,
To show yourself your father's son in deed
More than in words?

LAERTES

To cut his throat i' the church.

KING CLAUDIUS

No place, indeed, should murder sanctuarize;
Revenge should have no bounds. But, good Laertes,
Will you do this, keep close within your chamber.
Hamlet return'd shall know you are come home:
We'll put on those shall praise your excellence
And set a double varnish on the fame
The Frenchman gave you, bring you in fine together
And wager on your heads: he, being remiss,
Most generous and free from all contriving,
Will not peruse the foils; so that, with ease,
Or with a little shuffling, you may choose
A sword unbated, and in a pass of practise
Requite him for your father.

LAERTES

I will do't:
And, for that purpose, I'll anoint my sword.
I bought an unction of a mountebank,
So mortal that, but dip a knife in it,
Where it draws blood no cataplasm so rare,
Collected from all simples that have virtue
Under the moon, can save the thing from death
That is but scratch'd withal: I'll touch my point
With this contagion, that, if I gall him slightly,

It may be death.
KING CLAUDIUS
    Let's further think of this;
    Weigh what convenience both of time and means
    May fit us to our shape: if this should fail,
    And that our drift look through our bad performance,
    'Twere better not assay'd: therefore this project
    Should have a back or second, that might hold,
    If this should blast in proof. Soft! let me see:
    We'll make a solemn wager on your cunnings: I ha't.
    When in your motion you are hot and dry--
    As make your bouts more violent to that end--
    And that he calls for drink, I'll have prepared him
    A chalice for the nonce, whereon but sipping,
    If he by chance escape your venom'd stuck,
    Our purpose may hold there.

Enter QUEEN GERTRUDE

    How now, sweet queen!
QUEEN GERTRUDE
    One woe doth tread upon another's heel,
    So fast they follow; your sister's drown'd, Laertes.
LAERTES
    Drown'd! O, where?
QUEEN GERTRUDE
    There is a willow grows aslant a brook,
    That shows his hoar leaves in the glassy stream;
    There with fantastic garlands did she come
    Of crow-flowers, nettles, daisies, and long purples
    That liberal shepherds give a grosser name,
    But our cold maids do dead men's fingers call them:
    There, on the pendent boughs her coronet weeds
    Clambering to hang, an envious sliver broke;
    When down her weedy trophies and herself

Fell in the weeping brook. Her clothes spread wide;
And, mermaid-like, awhile they bore her up:
Which time she chanted snatches of old tunes;
As one incapable of her own distress,
Or like a creature native and indued
Unto that element: but long it could not be
Till that her garments, heavy with their drink,
Pull'd the poor wretch from her melodious lay
To muddy death.

LAERTES

Alas, then, she is drown'd?

QUEEN GERTRUDE

Drown'd, drown'd.

LAERTES

Too much of water hast thou, poor Ophelia,
And therefore I forbid my tears: but yet
It is our trick; nature her custom holds,
Let shame say what it will: when these are gone,
The woman will be out. Adieu, my lord:
I have a speech of fire, that fain would blaze,
But that this folly douts it.

Exit

KING CLAUDIUS

Let's follow, Gertrude:
How much I had to do to calm his rage!
Now fear I this will give it start again;
Therefore let's follow.

Exeunt

ACT V

SCENE I.

A churchyard.

Enter two Clowns, with spades, & c

First Clown
Is she to be buried in Christian burial that
wilfully seeks her own salvation?
Second Clown
I tell thee she is: and therefore make her grave
straight: the crowner hath sat on her, and finds it
Christian burial.
First Clown
How can that be, unless she drowned herself in her
own defence?
Second Clown
Why, 'tis found so.
First Clown
It must be 'se offendendo;' it cannot be else. For
here lies the point: if I drown myself wittingly,
it argues an act: and an act hath three branches: it
is, to act, to do, to perform: argal, she drowned
herself wittingly.
Second Clown
Nay, but hear you, goodman delver,--
First Clown
Give me leave. Here lies the water; good: here
stands the man; good; if the man go to this water,
and drown himself, it is, will he, nill he, he
goes,--mark you that; but if the water come to him
and drown him, he drowns not himself: argal, he

that is not guilty of his own death shortens not his own
life.

Second Clown

But is this law?

First Clown

Ay, marry, is't; crowner's quest law.

Second Clown

Will you ha' the truth on't? If this had not been
a gentlewoman, she should have been buried out o'
Christian burial.

First Clown

Why, there thou say'st: and the more pity that
great folk should have countenance in this world to
drown or hang themselves, more than their even
Christian. Come, my spade. There is no ancient
gentleman but gardeners, ditchers, and grave-makers:
they hold up Adam's profession.

Second Clown

Was he a gentleman?

First Clown

He was the first that ever bore arms.

Second Clown

Why, he had none.

First Clown

What, art a heathen? How dost thou understand the
Scripture? The Scripture says 'Adam digged:'
could he dig without arms? I'll put another
question to thee: if thou answerest me not to the
purpose, confess thyself--

Second Clown

Go to.

First Clown

What is he that builds stronger than either the
mason, the shipwright, or the carpenter?

Second Clown

The gallows-maker; for that frame outlives a
thousand tenants.

First Clown

I like thy wit well, in good faith: the gallows
does well; but how does it well? it does well to
those that do in: now thou dost ill to say the
gallows is built stronger than the church: argal,
the gallows may do well to thee. To't again, come.

Second Clown

'Who builds stronger than a mason, a shipwright, or
a carpenter?'

First Clown

Ay, tell me that, and unyoke.

Second Clown

Marry, now I can tell.

First Clown

To't.

Second Clown

Mass, I cannot tell.

Enter HAMLET and HORATIO, at a distance

First Clown

Cudgel thy brains no more about it, for your dull
ass will not mend his pace with beating; and, when
you are asked this question next, say 'a
grave-maker: 'the houses that he makes last till
doomsday. Go, get thee to Yaughan: fetch me a
stoup of liquor.

Exit Second Clown

He digs and sings

In youth, when I did love, did love,
Methought it was very sweet,
To contract, O, the time, for, ah, my behove,
O, methought, there was nothing meet.
HAMLET
Has this fellow no feeling of his business, that he
sings at grave-making?
HORATIO
Custom hath made it in him a property of easiness.
HAMLET
'Tis e'en so: the hand of little employment hath
the daintier sense.
First Clown
[Sings]
But age, with his stealing steps,
Hath claw'd me in his clutch,
And hath shipped me intil the land,
As if I had never been such.

Throws up a skull

HAMLET
That skull had a tongue in it, and could sing once:
how the knave jowls it to the ground, as if it were
Cain's jaw-bone, that did the first murder! It
might be the pate of a politician, which this ass
now o'er-reaches; one that would circumvent God,
might it not?
HORATIO
It might, my lord.
HAMLET
Or of a courtier; which could say 'Good morrow,
sweet lord! How dost thou, good lord?' This might
be my lord such-a-one, that praised my lord

such-a-one's horse, when he meant to beg it; might it
not?

HORATIO

Ay, my lord.

HAMLET

Why, e'en so: and now my Lady Worm's; chapless, and
knocked about the mazzard with a sexton's spade:
here's fine revolution, an we had the trick to
see't. Did these bones cost no more the breeding,
but to play at loggats with 'em? mine ache to think on't.

First Clown

[Sings]
A pick-axe, and a spade, a spade,
For and a shrouding sheet:
O, a pit of clay for to be made
For such a guest is meet.

Throws up another skull

HAMLET

There's another: why may not that be the skull of a
lawyer? Where be his quiddities now, his quillets,
his cases, his tenures, and his tricks? why does he
suffer this rude knave now to knock him about the
sconce with a dirty shovel, and will not tell him of
his action of battery? Hum! This fellow might be
in's time a great buyer of land, with his statutes,
his recognizances, his fines, his double vouchers,
his recoveries: is this the fine of his fines, and
the recovery of his recoveries, to have his fine
pate full of fine dirt? will his vouchers vouch him
no more of his purchases, and double ones too, than
the length and breadth of a pair of indentures? The
very conveyances of his lands will hardly lie in

this box; and must the inheritor himself have no more,
ha?

HORATIO

Not a jot more, my lord.

HAMLET

Is not parchment made of sheepskins?

HORATIO

Ay, my lord, and of calf-skins too.

HAMLET

They are sheep and calves which seek out assurance
in that. I will speak to this fellow. Whose
grave's this, sirrah?

First Clown

Mine, sir.

Sings

O, a pit of clay for to be made
For such a guest is meet.

HAMLET

I think it be thine, indeed; for thou liest in't.

First Clown

You lie out on't, sir, and therefore it is not
yours: for my part, I do not lie in't, and yet it is mine.

HAMLET

'Thou dost lie in't, to be in't and say it is thine:
'tis for the dead, not for the quick; therefore thou liest.

First Clown

'Tis a quick lie, sir; 'twill away gain, from me to
you.

HAMLET

What man dost thou dig it for?

First Clown

For no man, sir.

HAMLET

What woman, then?

First Clown

For none, neither.

HAMLET

Who is to be buried in't?

First Clown

One that was a woman, sir; but, rest her soul, she's dead.

HAMLET

How absolute the knave is! we must speak by the
card, or equivocation will undo us. By the Lord,
Horatio, these three years I have taken a note of
it; the age is grown so picked that the toe of the
peasant comes so near the heel of the courtier, he
gaffs his kibe. How long hast thou been a
grave-maker?

First Clown

Of all the days i' the year, I came to't that day
that our last king Hamlet overcame Fortinbras.

HAMLET

How long is that since?

First Clown

Cannot you tell that? every fool can tell that: it
was the very day that young Hamlet was born; he that
is mad, and sent into England.

HAMLET

Ay, marry, why was he sent into England?

First Clown

Why, because he was mad: he shall recover his wits
there; or, if he do not, it's no great matter there.

HAMLET

Why?

First Clown

'Twill, a not be seen in him there; there the men
are as mad as he.

HAMLET
How came he mad?
First Clown
Very strangely, they say.
HAMLET
How strangely?
First Clown
Faith, e'en with losing his wits.
HAMLET
Upon what ground?
First Clown
Why, here in Denmark: I have been sexton here, man
and boy, thirty years.
HAMLET
How long will a man lie i' the earth ere he rot?
First Clown
I' faith, if he be not rotten before he die--as we
have many pocky corses now-a-days, that will scarce
hold the laying in--he will last you some eight year
or nine year: a tanner will last you nine year.
HAMLET
Why he more than another?
First Clown
Why, sir, his hide is so tanned with his trade, that
he will keep out water a great while; and your water
is a sore decayer of your whoreson dead body.
Here's a skull now; this skull has lain in the earth
three and twenty years.
HAMLET
Whose was it?
First Clown
A whoreson mad fellow's it was: whose do you think it
was?
HAMLET

Nay, I know not.

First Clown

A pestilence on him for a mad rogue! a' poured a
flagon of Rhenish on my head once. This same skull,
sir, was Yorick's skull, the king's jester.

HAMLET

This?

First Clown

E'en that.

HAMLET

Let me see.

Takes the skull

Alas, poor Yorick! I knew him, Horatio: a fellow
of infinite jest, of most excellent fancy: he hath
borne me on his back a thousand times; and now, how
abhorred in my imagination it is! my gorge rims at
it. Here hung those lips that I have kissed I know
not how oft. Where be your gibes now? your
gambols? your songs? your flashes of merriment,
that were wont to set the table on a roar? Not one
now, to mock your own grinning? quite chap-fallen?
Now get you to my lady's chamber, and tell her, let
her paint an inch thick, to this favour she must
come; make her laugh at that. Prithee, Horatio, tell
me one thing.

HORATIO

What's that, my lord?

HAMLET

Dost thou think Alexander looked o' this fashion i'
the earth?

HORATIO

E'en so.

HAMLET

And smelt so? pah!

Puts down the skull

HORATIO
E'en so, my lord.
HAMLET
To what base uses we may return, Horatio! Why may
not imagination trace the noble dust of Alexander,
till he find it stopping a bung-hole?
HORATIO
'Twere to consider too curiously, to consider so.
HAMLET
No, faith, not a jot; but to follow him thither with
modesty enough, and likelihood to lead it: as
thus: Alexander died, Alexander was buried,
Alexander returneth into dust; the dust is earth; of
earth we make loam; and why of that loam, whereto he
was converted, might they not stop a beer-barrel?
Imperious Caesar, dead and turn'd to clay,
Might stop a hole to keep the wind away:
O, that that earth, which kept the world in awe,
Should patch a wall to expel the winter flaw!
But soft! but soft! aside: here comes the king.

Enter Priest, & c. in procession; the Corpse of OPHELIA,
LAERTES and Mourners following; KING CLAUDIUS,
QUEEN GERTRUDE, their trains, & c

The queen, the courtiers: who is this they follow?
And with such maimed rites? This doth betoken
The corse they follow did with desperate hand
Fordo its own life: 'twas of some estate.
Couch we awhile, and mark.

Retiring with HORATIO

LAERTES
  What ceremony else?
HAMLET
  That is Laertes,
  A very noble youth: mark.
LAERTES
  What ceremony else?
First Priest
  Her obsequies have been as far enlarged
  As we have warrantise: her death was doubtful;
  And, but that great command o'ersways the order,
  She should in ground unsanctified have lodged
  Till the last trumpet: for charitable prayers,
  Shards, flints and pebbles should be thrown on her;
  Yet here she is allow'd her virgin crants,
  Her maiden strewments and the bringing home
  Of bell and burial.
LAERTES
  Must there no more be done?
First Priest
  No more be done:
  We should profane the service of the dead
  To sing a requiem and such rest to her
  As to peace-parted souls.
LAERTES
  Lay her i' the earth:
  And from her fair and unpolluted flesh
  May violets spring! I tell thee, churlish priest,
  A ministering angel shall my sister be,
  When thou liest howling.
HAMLET
  What, the fair Ophelia!
QUEEN GERTRUDE

Sweets to the sweet: farewell!

Scattering flowers

I hoped thou shouldst have been my Hamlet's wife;
I thought thy bride-bed to have deck'd, sweet maid,
And not have strew'd thy grave.
LAERTES
O, treble woe
Fall ten times treble on that cursed head,
Whose wicked deed thy most ingenious sense
Deprived thee of! Hold off the earth awhile,
Till I have caught her once more in mine arms:

Leaps into the grave

Now pile your dust upon the quick and dead,
Till of this flat a mountain you have made,
To o'ertop old Pelion, or the skyish head
Of blue Olympus.
HAMLET
[Advancing] What is he whose grief
Bears such an emphasis? whose phrase of sorrow
Conjures the wandering stars, and makes them stand
Like wonder-wounded hearers? This is I,
Hamlet the Dane.

Leaps into the grave

LAERTES
The devil take thy soul!

Grappling with him

HAMLET
Thou pray'st not well.
I prithee, take thy fingers from my throat;

154

For, though I am not splenitive and rash,
Yet have I something in me dangerous,
Which let thy wiseness fear: hold off thy hand.
KING CLAUDIUS
Pluck them asunder.
QUEEN GERTRUDE
Hamlet, Hamlet!
All
Gentlemen,--
HORATIO
Good my lord, be quiet.

The Attendants part them, and they come out of the grave

HAMLET
Why I will fight with him upon this theme
Until my eyelids will no longer wag.
QUEEN GERTRUDE
O my son, what theme?
HAMLET
I loved Ophelia: forty thousand brothers
Could not, with all their quantity of love,
Make up my sum. What wilt thou do for her?
KING CLAUDIUS
O, he is mad, Laertes.
QUEEN GERTRUDE
For love of God, forbear him.
HAMLET
'Swounds, show me what thou'lt do:
Woo't weep? woo't fight? woo't fast? woo't tear thyself?
Woo't drink up eisel? eat a crocodile?
I'll do't. Dost thou come here to whine?
To outface me with leaping in her grave?
Be buried quick with her, and so will I:
And, if thou prate of mountains, let them throw

Millions of acres on us, till our ground,
Singeing his pate against the burning zone,
Make Ossa like a wart! Nay, an thou'lt mouth,
I'll rant as well as thou.

QUEEN GERTRUDE
This is mere madness:
And thus awhile the fit will work on him;
Anon, as patient as the female dove,
When that her golden couplets are disclosed,
His silence will sit drooping.

HAMLET
Hear you, sir;
What is the reason that you use me thus?
I loved you ever: but it is no matter;
Let Hercules himself do what he may,
The cat will mew and dog will have his day.

Exit

KING CLAUDIUS
I pray you, good Horatio, wait upon him.

Exit HORATIO

To LAERTES

Strengthen your patience in our last night's speech;
We'll put the matter to the present push.
Good Gertrude, set some watch over your son.
This grave shall have a living monument:
An hour of quiet shortly shall we see;
Till then, in patience our proceeding be.

Exeunt

SCENE II.

A hall in the castle.

Enter HAMLET and HORATIO

HAMLET

    So much for this, sir: now shall you see the other;

    You do remember all the circumstance?

HORATIO

    Remember it, my lord?

HAMLET

    Sir, in my heart there was a kind of fighting,

    That would not let me sleep: methought I lay

    Worse than the mutines in the bilboes. Rashly,

    And praised be rashness for it, let us know,

    Our indiscretion sometimes serves us well,

    When our deep plots do pall: and that should teach us

    There's a divinity that shapes our ends,

    Rough-hew them how we will,--

HORATIO

    That is most certain.

HAMLET

    Up from my cabin,

    My sea-gown scarf'd about me, in the dark

    Groped I to find out them; had my desire.

    Finger'd their packet, and in fine withdrew

    To mine own room again; making so bold,

    My fears forgetting manners, to unseal

    Their grand commission; where I found, Horatio,--

    O royal knavery!--an exact command,

    Larded with many several sorts of reasons

    Importing Denmark's health and England's too,

    With, ho! such bugs and goblins in my life,

    That, on the supervise, no leisure bated,

    No, not to stay the grinding of the axe,

My head should be struck off.

HORATIO

Is't possible?

HAMLET

Here's the commission: read it at more leisure.
But wilt thou hear me how I did proceed?

HORATIO

I beseech you.

HAMLET

Being thus be-netted round with villanies,--
Ere I could make a prologue to my brains,
They had begun the play--I sat me down,
Devised a new commission, wrote it fair:
I once did hold it, as our statists do,
A baseness to write fair and labour'd much
How to forget that learning, but, sir, now
It did me yeoman's service: wilt thou know
The effect of what I wrote?

HORATIO

Ay, good my lord.

HAMLET

An earnest conjuration from the king,
As England was his faithful tributary,
As love between them like the palm might flourish,
As peace should stiff her wheaten garland wear
And stand a comma 'tween their amities,
And many such-like 'As'es of great charge,
That, on the view and knowing of these contents,
Without debatement further, more or less,
He should the bearers put to sudden death,
Not shriving-time allow'd.

HORATIO

How was this seal'd?

HAMLET

Why, even in that was heaven ordinant.
I had my father's signet in my purse,
Which was the model of that Danish seal;
Folded the writ up in form of the other,
Subscribed it, gave't the impression, placed it safely,
The changeling never known. Now, the next day
Was our sea-fight; and what to this was sequent
Thou know'st already.

HORATIO

So Guildenstern and Rosencrantz go to't.

HAMLET

Why, man, they did make love to this employment;
They are not near my conscience; their defeat
Does by their own insinuation grow:
'Tis dangerous when the baser nature comes
Between the pass and fell incensed points
Of mighty opposites.

HORATIO

Why, what a king is this!

HAMLET

Does it not, think'st thee, stand me now upon--
He that hath kill'd my king and whored my mother,
Popp'd in between the election and my hopes,
Thrown out his angle for my proper life,
And with such cozenage--is't not perfect conscience,
To quit him with this arm? and is't not to be damn'd,
To let this canker of our nature come
In further evil?

HORATIO

It must be shortly known to him from England
What is the issue of the business there.

HAMLET

It will be short: the interim is mine;
And a man's life's no more than to say 'One.'

But I am very sorry, good Horatio,
That to Laertes I forgot myself;
For, by the image of my cause, I see
The portraiture of his: I'll court his favours.
But, sure, the bravery of his grief did put me
Into a towering passion.
HORATIO
Peace! who comes here?

Enter OSRIC

OSRIC
Your lordship is right welcome back to Denmark.
HAMLET
I humbly thank you, sir. Dost know this water-fly?
HORATIO
No, my good lord.
HAMLET
Thy state is the more gracious; for 'tis a vice to
know him. He hath much land, and fertile: let a
beast be lord of beasts, and his crib shall stand at
the king's mess: 'tis a chough; but, as I say,
spacious in the possession of dirt.
OSRIC
Sweet lord, if your lordship were at leisure, I
should impart a thing to you from his majesty.
HAMLET
I will receive it, sir, with all diligence of
spirit. Put your bonnet to his right use; 'tis for the head.
OSRIC
I thank your lordship, it is very hot.
HAMLET
No, believe me, 'tis very cold; the wind is
northerly.
OSRIC

It is indifferent cold, my lord, indeed.
HAMLET
But yet methinks it is very sultry and hot for my
complexion.
OSRIC
Exceedingly, my lord; it is very sultry,--as
'twere,--I cannot tell how. But, my lord, his
majesty bade me signify to you that he has laid a
great wager on your head: sir, this is the matter,--
HAMLET
I beseech you, remember--

HAMLET moves him to put on his hat

OSRIC
Nay, good my lord; for mine ease, in good faith.
Sir, here is newly come to court Laertes; believe
me, an absolute gentleman, full of most excellent
differences, of very soft society and great showing:
indeed, to speak feelingly of him, he is the card or
calendar of gentry, for you shall find in him the
continent of what part a gentleman would see.
HAMLET
Sir, his definement suffers no perdition in you;
though, I know, to divide him inventorially would
dizzy the arithmetic of memory, and yet but yaw
neither, in respect of his quick sail. But, in the
verity of extolment, I take him to be a soul of
great article; and his infusion of such dearth and
rareness, as, to make true diction of him, his
semblable is his mirror; and who else would trace
him, his umbrage, nothing more.
OSRIC
Your lordship speaks most infallibly of him.
HAMLET

The concernancy, sir? why do we wrap the gentleman
in our more rawer breath?

OSRIC

Sir?

HORATIO

Is't not possible to understand in another tongue?
You will do't, sir, really.

HAMLET

What imports the nomination of this gentleman?

OSRIC

Of Laertes?

HORATIO

His purse is empty already; all's golden words are spent.

HAMLET

Of him, sir.

OSRIC

I know you are not ignorant--

HAMLET

I would you did, sir; yet, in faith, if you did,
it would not much approve me. Well, sir?

OSRIC

You are not ignorant of what excellence Laertes is--

HAMLET

I dare not confess that, lest I should compare with
him in excellence; but, to know a man well, were to
know himself.

OSRIC

I mean, sir, for his weapon; but in the imputation
laid on him by them, in his meed he's unfellowed.

HAMLET

What's his weapon?

OSRIC

Rapier and dagger.

HAMLET

That's two of his weapons: but, well.

OSRIC

    The king, sir, hath wagered with him six Barbary
    horses: against the which he has imponed, as I take
    it, six French rapiers and poniards, with their
    assigns, as girdle, hangers, and so: three of the
    carriages, in faith, are very dear to fancy, very
    responsive to the hilts, most delicate carriages,
    and of very liberal conceit.

HAMLET

    What call you the carriages?

HORATIO

    I knew you must be edified by the margent ere you had
    done.

OSRIC

    The carriages, sir, are the hangers.

HAMLET

    The phrase would be more german to the matter, if we
    could carry cannon by our sides: I would it might
    be hangers till then. But, on: six Barbary horses
    against six French swords, their assigns, and three
    liberal-conceited carriages; that's the French bet
    against the Danish. Why is this 'imponed,' as you call it?

OSRIC

    The king, sir, hath laid, that in a dozen passes
    between yourself and him, he shall not exceed you
    three hits: he hath laid on twelve for nine; and it
    would come to immediate trial, if your lordship
    would vouchsafe the answer.

HAMLET

    How if I answer 'no'?

OSRIC

    I mean, my lord, the opposition of your person in trial.

HAMLET

Sir, I will walk here in the hall: if it please his
majesty, 'tis the breathing time of day with me; let
the foils be brought, the gentleman willing, and the
king hold his purpose, I will win for him an I can;
if not, I will gain nothing but my shame and the odd
hits.

OSRIC

Shall I re-deliver you e'en so?

HAMLET

To this effect, sir; after what flourish your nature will.

OSRIC

I commend my duty to your lordship.

HAMLET

Yours, yours.

Exit OSRIC

He does well to commend it himself; there are no
tongues else for's turn.

HORATIO

This lapwing runs away with the shell on his head.

HAMLET

He did comply with his dug, before he sucked it.
Thus has he--and many more of the same bevy that I
know the dressy age dotes on--only got the tune of
the time and outward habit of encounter; a kind of
yesty collection, which carries them through and
through the most fond and winnowed opinions; and do
but blow them to their trial, the bubbles are out.

Enter a Lord

Lord

My lord, his majesty commended him to you by young
Osric, who brings back to him that you attend him in

the hall: he sends to know if your pleasure hold to
play with Laertes, or that you will take longer time.

HAMLET

I am constant to my purpose; they follow the king's
pleasure: if his fitness speaks, mine is ready; now
or whensoever, provided I be so able as now.

Lord

The king and queen and all are coming down.

HAMLET

In happy time.

Lord

The queen desires you to use some gentle
entertainment to Laertes before you fall to play.

HAMLET

She well instructs me.

Exit Lord

HORATIO

You will lose this wager, my lord.

HAMLET

I do not think so: since he went into France, I
have been in continual practise: I shall win at the
odds. But thou wouldst not think how ill all's here
about my heart: but it is no matter.

HORATIO

Nay, good my lord,--

HAMLET

It is but foolery; but it is such a kind of
gain-giving, as would perhaps trouble a woman.

HORATIO

If your mind dislike any thing, obey it: I will
forestall their repair hither, and say you are not
fit.

HAMLET

Not a whit, we defy augury: there's a special
providence in the fall of a sparrow. If it be now,
'tis not to come; if it be not to come, it will be
now; if it be not now, yet it will come: the
readiness is all: since no man has aught of what he
leaves, what is't to leave betimes?

Enter KING CLAUDIUS, QUEEN GERTRUDE, LAERTES,
Lords, OSRIC, and Attendants with foils, & c

KING CLAUDIUS

Come, Hamlet, come, and take this hand from me.

KING CLAUDIUS puts LAERTES' hand into HAMLET's

HAMLET

Give me your pardon, sir: I've done you wrong;
But pardon't, as you are a gentleman.
This presence knows,
And you must needs have heard, how I am punish'd
With sore distraction. What I have done,
That might your nature, honour and exception
Roughly awake, I here proclaim was madness.
Was't Hamlet wrong'd Laertes? Never Hamlet:
If Hamlet from himself be ta'en away,
And when he's not himself does wrong Laertes,
Then Hamlet does it not, Hamlet denies it.
Who does it, then? His madness: if't be so,
Hamlet is of the faction that is wrong'd;
His madness is poor Hamlet's enemy.
Sir, in this audience,
Let my disclaiming from a purposed evil
Free me so far in your most generous thoughts,
That I have shot mine arrow o'er the house,
And hurt my brother.

LAERTES

    I am satisfied in nature,

    Whose motive, in this case, should stir me most

    To my revenge: but in my terms of honour

    I stand aloof; and will no reconcilement,

    Till by some elder masters, of known honour,

    I have a voice and precedent of peace,

    To keep my name ungored. But till that time,

    I do receive your offer'd love like love,

    And will not wrong it.

HAMLET

    I embrace it freely;

    And will this brother's wager frankly play.

    Give us the foils. Come on.

LAERTES

    Come, one for me.

HAMLET

    I'll be your foil, Laertes: in mine ignorance

    Your skill shall, like a star i' the darkest night,

    Stick fiery off indeed.

LAERTES

    You mock me, sir.

HAMLET

    No, by this hand.

KING CLAUDIUS

    Give them the foils, young Osric. Cousin Hamlet,

    You know the wager?

HAMLET

    Very well, my lord

    Your grace hath laid the odds o' the weaker side.

KING CLAUDIUS

    I do not fear it; I have seen you both:

    But since he is better'd, we have therefore odds.

LAERTES

This is too heavy, let me see another.
HAMLET
This likes me well. These foils have all a length?

They prepare to play

OSRIC
Ay, my good lord.
KING CLAUDIUS
Set me the stoops of wine upon that table.
If Hamlet give the first or second hit,
Or quit in answer of the third exchange,
Let all the battlements their ordnance fire:
The king shall drink to Hamlet's better breath;
And in the cup an union shall he throw,
Richer than that which four successive kings
In Denmark's crown have worn. Give me the cups;
And let the kettle to the trumpet speak,
The trumpet to the cannoneer without,
The cannons to the heavens, the heavens to earth,
'Now the king dunks to Hamlet.' Come, begin:
And you, the judges, bear a wary eye.
HAMLET
Come on, sir.
LAERTES
Come, my lord.

They play

HAMLET
One.
LAERTES
No.
HAMLET
Judgment.

OSRIC
A hit, a very palpable hit.
LAERTES
Well; again.
KING CLAUDIUS
Stay; give me drink. Hamlet, this pearl is thine;
Here's to thy health.

Trumpets sound, and cannon shot off within

Give him the cup.
HAMLET
I'll play this bout first; set it by awhile. Come.

They play

Another hit; what say you?
LAERTES
A touch, a touch, I do confess.
KING CLAUDIUS
Our son shall win.
QUEEN GERTRUDE
He's fat, and scant of breath.
Here, Hamlet, take my napkin, rub thy brows;
The queen carouses to thy fortune, Hamlet.
HAMLET
Good madam!
KING CLAUDIUS
Gertrude, do not drink.
QUEEN GERTRUDE
I will, my lord; I pray you, pardon me.
KING CLAUDIUS
[Aside] It is the poison'd cup: it is too late.
HAMLET
I dare not drink yet, madam; by and by.

QUEEN GERTRUDE
  Come, let me wipe thy face.
LAERTES
  My lord, I'll hit him now.
KING CLAUDIUS
  I do not think't.
LAERTES
  [Aside] And yet 'tis almost 'gainst my conscience.
HAMLET
  Come, for the third, Laertes: you but dally;
  I pray you, pass with your best violence;
  I am afeard you make a wanton of me.
LAERTES
  Say you so? come on.

They play

OSRIC
  Nothing, neither way.
LAERTES
  Have at you now!

*LAERTES wounds HAMLET; then in scuffling, they change
rapiers, and HAMLET wounds LAERTES*

KING CLAUDIUS
  Part them; they are incensed.
HAMLET
  Nay, come, again.

QUEEN GERTRUDE falls

OSRIC
  Look to the queen there, ho!
HORATIO
  They bleed on both sides. How is it, my lord?

OSRIC
How is't, Laertes?
LAERTES
Why, as a woodcock to mine own springe, Osric;
I am justly kill'd with mine own treachery.
HAMLET
How does the queen?
KING CLAUDIUS
She swounds to see them bleed.
QUEEN GERTRUDE
No, no, the drink, the drink,--O my dear Hamlet,--
The drink, the drink! I am poison'd.

Dies

HAMLET
O villany! Ho! let the door be lock'd:
Treachery! Seek it out.
LAERTES
It is here, Hamlet: Hamlet, thou art slain;
No medicine in the world can do thee good;
In thee there is not half an hour of life;
The treacherous instrument is in thy hand,
Unbated and envenom'd: the foul practise
Hath turn'd itself on me lo, here I lie,
Never to rise again: thy mother's poison'd:
I can no more: the king, the king's to blame.
HAMLET
The point!--envenom'd too!
Then, venom, to thy work.

Stabs KING CLAUDIUS

All
Treason! treason!

KING CLAUDIUS
    O, yet defend me, friends; I am but hurt.
HAMLET
    Here, thou incestuous, murderous, damned Dane,
    Drink off this potion. Is thy union here?
    Follow my mother.

KING CLAUDIUS dies

LAERTES
    He is justly served;
    It is a poison temper'd by himself.
    Exchange forgiveness with me, noble Hamlet:
    Mine and my father's death come not upon thee,
    Nor thine on me.

Dies

HAMLET
    Heaven make thee free of it! I follow thee.
    I am dead, Horatio. Wretched queen, adieu!
    You that look pale and tremble at this chance,
    That are but mutes or audience to this act,
    Had I but time--as this fell sergeant, death,
    Is strict in his arrest--O, I could tell you--
    But let it be. Horatio, I am dead;
    Thou livest; report me and my cause aright
    To the unsatisfied.
HORATIO
    Never believe it:
    I am more an antique Roman than a Dane:
    Here's yet some liquor left.
HAMLET
    As thou'rt a man,
    Give me the cup: let go; by heaven, I'll have't.

O good Horatio, what a wounded name,
Things standing thus unknown, shall live behind me!
If thou didst ever hold me in thy heart
Absent thee from felicity awhile,
And in this harsh world draw thy breath in pain,
To tell my story.

March afar off, and shot within

What warlike noise is this?

OSRIC

Young Fortinbras, with conquest come from Poland,
To the ambassadors of England gives
This warlike volley.

HAMLET

O, I die, Horatio;
The potent poison quite o'er-crows my spirit:
I cannot live to hear the news from England;
But I do prophesy the election lights
On Fortinbras: he has my dying voice;
So tell him, with the occurrents, more and less,
Which have solicited. The rest is silence.

Dies

HORATIO

Now cracks a noble heart. Good night sweet prince:
And flights of angels sing thee to thy rest!
Why does the drum come hither?
March within

Enter FORTINBRAS, the English Ambassadors, and others

PRINCE FORTINBRAS

Where is this sight?

HORATIO
> What is it ye would see?
> If aught of woe or wonder, cease your search.

PRINCE FORTINBRAS
> This quarry cries on havoc. O proud death,
> What feast is toward in thine eternal cell,
> That thou so many princes at a shot
> So bloodily hast struck?

First Ambassador
> The sight is dismal;
> And our affairs from England come too late:
> The ears are senseless that should give us hearing,
> To tell him his commandment is fulfill'd,
> That Rosencrantz and Guildenstern are dead:
> Where should we have our thanks?

HORATIO
> Not from his mouth,
> Had it the ability of life to thank you:
> He never gave commandment for their death.
> But since, so jump upon this bloody question,
> You from the Polack wars, and you from England,
> Are here arrived give order that these bodies
> High on a stage be placed to the view;
> And let me speak to the yet unknowing world
> How these things came about: so shall you hear
> Of carnal, bloody, and unnatural acts,
> Of accidental judgments, casual slaughters,
> Of deaths put on by cunning and forced cause,
> And, in this upshot, purposes mistook
> Fall'n on the inventors' reads: all this can I
> Truly deliver.

PRINCE FORTINBRAS
> Let us haste to hear it,
> And call the noblest to the audience.

For me, with sorrow I embrace my fortune:
I have some rights of memory in this kingdom,
Which now to claim my vantage doth invite me.

HORATIO

Of that I shall have also cause to speak,
And from his mouth whose voice will draw on more;
But let this same be presently perform'd,
Even while men's minds are wild; lest more mischance
On plots and errors, happen.

PRINCE FORTINBRAS

Let four captains
Bear Hamlet, like a soldier, to the stage;
For he was likely, had he been put on,
To have proved most royally: and, for his passage,
The soldiers' music and the rites of war
Speak loudly for him.
Take up the bodies: such a sight as this
Becomes the field, but here shows much amiss.
Go, bid the soldiers shoot.

*A dead march. Exeunt, bearing off the dead bodies; after
which a peal of ordnance is shot off*

Biography

A Short Life of Edward de Vere, 17th Earl of Oxford

by Dr. Kevin Gilvary, President
The de Vere Society

He was born on 12 April 1550 at Castle Hedingham, his family's ancestral home. His father, John de Vere, 16th Earl, was Lord Great Chamberlain and attended the coronations of both Mary and Elizabeth Tudor. His mother was Margaret Golding. Edward was 11 when, in 1561, Queen Elizabeth visited Hedingham for four days of masques, feasting and entertainments. When his father died in 1562, young Oxford left to become, like Bertram in *All's Well that Ends Well*, a ward of the Crown under the guardianship of William Cecil, the Queen's private secretary (later Lord Burghley, Lord Treasurer). His mother married Charles Tyrrell and seems to have passed out of the boy's life. His sister Mary went to live with her stepfather and the siblings were not reunited for some years.

According to a curriculum in Cecil's own hand, Edward de Vere's daily studies included dancing, French, Latin, writing and drawing, cosmography, penmanship, riding, shooting, exercise and prayer. Edward de Vere showed a prodigious talent for scholarship from his early years, and we may ascribe his lifelong love of learning to the influence of two of his early tutors. The first was Sir Thomas Smith who was, perhaps, England's most respected Greek scholar and the former Cambridge tutor of Sir William Cecil. It was, no doubt, through Cecil's influence that Edward de Vere spent some time living in the household of Smith in his early years, during which time he spent about five months at Smith's alma mater, Queens' College, Cambridge. Smith was a scholar of widely varied interests – this was reflected in his 400-volume library, some of which is still extant at Cambridge. De Vere's other tutor was Laurence Nowell, who was not only an accomplished cartographer but was also England's premier scholar of Anglo-Saxon literature – it was Nowell who possessed the only known copy of *Beowulf*.

Another important influence on Edward de Vere's early studies was his maternal uncle Arthur Golding, an officer in the Court of Wards under Cecil, who is credited with the translation of Ovid's *Metamorphoses*, published in 1567, a book widely recognised as having a major influence on 'Shakespeare'.

Following on from his matriculation at Cambridge in November 1558, Edward was awarded an honorary MA by Cambridge during a Royal progress in August 1564, and another degree by Oxford University during a Royal progress in 1566. Edward de Vere then attended Gray's Inn to study law. One notable feature of the Elizabethan Inns of Court was a tradition of mounting dramatic productions and of hosting the various touring companies of players.

In 1570 he served in a military campaign in Scotland under the Earl of Sussex. By 1571, he was reported as a leading luminary of the Court and, for a time, a favourite of Queen Elizabeth. In December 1571 he married Anne Cecil, aged 15, daughter of his guardian. This was a dynastic marriage where all the advantage accrued to Cecil who, ennobled as Baron Burghley, had reduced the social gap between himself and the young Earl.

While Oxford was away on a Grand Tour of Europe, he heard that his daughter Elizabeth Vere had been born in July 1575. On his return in early 1576, he appeared to have been convinced that Elizabeth was not his child; consequently he became estranged from Anne for five years, and exiled himself from Court, taking up residence in the Savoy and concerning himself with literary and musical patronage.

Already, in 1573, *Cardanus Comfort* (the Consolations of Boethius) had been translated from Latin by Thomas Bedingfield and dedicated to Oxford; and published with a preface written by him. In 1576 an anthology, *A Paradise of Daintie Devices*, including several poems by Oxford, was published. These are juvenile works but already show affinities, in both style and thought, with those of the mature Shakespeare.

Oxford's Grand Tour had taken in Paris, Strasbourg, Venice, Genoa, Florence, Palermo and, on his way back through France, Rousillon – the setting for *Love's Labour's Lost*. Oxford spent the best part of a year travelling in Italy in 1576, and becoming involved with moneylenders. He came back to England fluent in Italian and well acquainted with the northern Italian cities, to be satirised by Gabriel Harvey as 'The Italian Earl'. On his way back his ship was attacked by pirates in the English Channel (cf. *Hamlet*). Fourteen of 'Shakespeare's' plays have Italian settings, in which he put his detailed knowledge of the country, beyond pure book knowledge, to good use.

1573 saw the birth of Henry Wriothesley, Earl of Southampton. Although history has not bequeathed to us any evidence of a direct relationship between the two men, in the relatively small world of the royal Court, they must have been acquainted with each other. The poems *Venus and Adonis* (1593) and *The Rape of Lucrece* (1594) were dedicated to Southampton. These were the first works to be published under the name 'Shakespeare' and for the next five years the records show the byline 'Shakespeare' to have been associated exclusively with these two poems. Plays under the name 'Shakespeare' did not appear in print until 1598, the year that Lord Burghley died.

In May 1577 Oxford invested in Frobisher's voyage in the ship *Edward Bonaventure*. Despite its name, the ship's voyage across the Atlantic in search of the North-West Passage lost money; consequently he was forced to sell three estates (cf. Hamlet's words 'I am but mad north-north-west' II.1.). In 1578 he invested in Frobisher's second expedition, which also lost money, forcing further sales of estates.

He was mentioned by Gabriel Harvey in an address to Queen Elizabeth in July 1578, as a prolific private poet and one 'whose countenance shakes spears'. In the same year John Lyly, Oxford's secretary, published *Euphues.The Anatomy of Wit*, followed in 1579 by *Euphues and his England*, dedicated to Oxford. These two books launched the fashion for 'Euphuism', a style characterized by high-flown language, satirized in *Love's Labour's Lost*.

In March 1581 Oxford's mistress, Anne Vavasour, who was one of Queen Elizabeth's Ladies of the Bedchamber, gave birth to a son. The lovers and their son were sent to the Tower by an infuriated Queen but swiftly released (cf. *Measure for Measure*). After his release, Oxford was wounded in a street-fight provoked by Thomas Knyvet, a kinsman of Anne Vavasour; affrays continued in the streets of London between the rival gangs of supporters for over a year (cf.*Romeo and Juliet*).

In December 1581 he resumed living with his long-suffering and devoted wife, and accepted Elizabeth

Vere as his child. Tragically, their only son died one day after his birth. Three more daughters followed, of whom Susan and Bridget survived.

In 1584, Robert Greene's *Gwydonius; the Card of Fancy* was dedicated to him, identifying him as a 'pre-eminent writer'. In 1586, when he was 36, he served on the tribunal which condemned Mary, Queen of Scots to execution.

In the same year, the Queen awarded Oxford an unconditional pension of £1,000 a year for life (about £500,000 at today's value). The motive for this uncharacteristic generosity on the part of the Queen remains a mystery – no accounting was required of Oxford. Her successor, King James I, continued to pay the pension. In reply to Sir Robert Cecil's request that Lord Sheffield's pension be increased, the King refused, saying, 'Great Oxford got no more . . .', leaving us to wonder why Great Oxford? His greatness does not seem to have resided in war or any of the known offices of State. Perhaps a clue can be found in a letter to Burghley, written in 1594, in which Edward de Vere seeks his favour in a matter involving what he describes as 'in mine office' and that this office is beholden to the Queen.

In 1589, George Puttenham published *The Arte of English Poesie* and this contains the most telling recognition of Edward de Vere's literary standing amongst his contemporaries: 'And in her Majesties time that now is are sprong up an other crew of Courtly makers Noble men and Gentlemen of her Majesties owne servantes, who have written excellently well as it would appeare if their doings could be found out and made publicke with the rest, of which number is first that noble Gentleman Edward Earle of Oxford.'

In 1588 his wife Anne, daughter of Lord Burghley, died and in extant letters written at this time, it is reported that Burghley is so incapacitated by grief over the death of his favourite daughter that he is incapable of conducting any Privy Council business.

Three years later, in 1591, Oxford married another of the Queen's Maids of Honour, Elizabeth Trentham, with whom he finally became the father of a male heir; Henry de Vere, 18th Earl of Oxford. Although there is evidence of his continued involvement in Court affairs, from the date of this marriage Edward de Vere's life at his new home at King's Place in Hackney is perhaps the most obscure of his entire life.

In 1594, his ship the *Edward Bonaventure* was wrecked in Bermuda (cf. *The Tempest*). In January 1595, Elizabeth Vere married William Stanley, 6th Earl of Derby, another literary earl who maintained his own company of players – many scholars believe that *A Midsummer Night's Dream* was written for these festivities which were attended by the whole royal Court.

On September 7 1598, Francis Meres' *Palladis Tamia* was registered for publication, naming Oxford as the 'best for comedy'. This is a vital document in Shakespearean history because it includes the first mention of 'Shakespeare' as a playwright, attributing twelve plays to him; until then Shakespeare's reputation had rested on the two narrative poems only.

Oxford suffered all his life from financial difficulties, much of which can be traced to the fact that Queen Elizabeth handed out the bulk of his estate to her favourite courtier the Earl of Leicester during Oxford's minority as a royal ward (estates which Oxford found almost impossible to reclaim), and the ruinous debt she placed upon him over his marriage to Anne Cecil. It is, however, notable that his new brother-in-law, the wealthy Staffordshire landowner and Knight of the Shire Francis Trentham, took over the management of Edward de

Vere's near-bankrupt estate from 1591 and gradually nursed it back to health so that, when Oxford died, all of his massive debts had been cleared.

On the Queen's death in 1603 Oxford wrote eloquently to Sir Robert Cecil, son and heir of Lord Burghley, of his 'great grief'. He wrote, 'In this common shipwreck, mine is above all the rest, who least regarded, though often comforted, she hath left to try my fortune among the alterations of time and chance'.

Oxford died in Hackney in 1604, cause unknown. Parish records state that he was buried in Hackney Church on July 6, but a family history by his first cousin Percival Golding, states 'Edward de Veer ... a man in mind and body absolutely accomplished with honorable endowments ... lieth buried at Westminster'. No record of such a burial can now be traced in Westminster Abbey, where there is a Vere family tomb.

The Aftermath of Oxford's life and death

During the winter season 1604-05, six of Shakespeare's plays were presented at Court by command of King James I. This has an air of commemoration. In 1609 the *Sonnets* were published in a pirated edition. The famous dedication describes the author as 'our ever-living', a phrase invariably used only of the dead.

In 1622 Henry Peacham published, in *The Compleat Gentelman*, a list of poets who made Elizabeth's reign a 'golden age'. Unaccountably, he omitted Shakespeare but placed the Earl of Oxford in first place in his list – perhaps he knew them to be the same person. This is unlike Meres who included them both – maybe one reason was because he didn't know Oxford and Shakespeare were the same person.

We do not know who instigated publication of the First Folio Edition of the Shakespeare plays in 1623, but there is no mention of any executor or relative of Shakspere of Stratford in connection with it. However, of the two brothers who financed it and to whom it was dedicated, one – Philip Earl of Montgomery – was the husband of Oxford's daughter Susan, while the other – William Earl of Pembroke – had once been a suitor for her sister Bridget. Pembroke was Lord Chamberlain, the supreme authority in the world of theatre, and thus in a position to decide which plays were to be published and which suppressed. We also know that Ben Jonson, who wrote much of the introductory material, was an intimate associate of the de Vere family after Oxford's death. The First Folio was therefore very much a family affair, but the family was not the one in Stratford-on-Avon.

An AfterVerse

For those with yet an interest
In strenuous debate
We've compiled a list of books and films
Your appetite to sate.
From this study clear your mind
Of doubt and all misgiving-
Who from us has long since gone
And who is ever-living.

Selected References & Bibliography
About the Author
Edward de Vere, 17th Earl of Oxford

Books

♦ Anderson, M. (2005). *Shakespeare by Another Name: The Life of Edward de Vere, Earl of Oxford, The Man who was Shakespeare.* New York: Gotham Books. *--A physicist by training with research interest in how evidence supports or negates a theory, Mark Anderson spent ten years investigating Edward de Vere as the author of Shake-speare's works.*

♦Farina, William. (2006). *De Vere as Shakespeare: An Oxfordian Reading of the Canon.* Jefferson, NC. McFarland & Company.

--Each of the plays and poems is individually assessed and explored in its own chapter, using the innumerable connections between the text itself and the life of its author, Edward de Vere.

♦ Looney, J. Thomas (2018). *Shakespeare Identified.* Cary, N.C. Veritas Publicaations.
--First published in 1920 this book began the modern Oxfordian movement. From reading it, Sigmund Freud became convinced and John Galsworthy called it "the best detective story I ever read."

♦ Ogburn, C. (1992). *The Mysterious William Shakespeare.* McLean (Va.): EPM.
--An in depth exploration and must read foundational book on the authorship question.

♦Sobran, Joseph. (1997). *Alias Shakespeare: Solving the Greatest Literary Mystery of All Time.*
New York; The Free Press, A Division of Simon & Schuster.
--A concise exploration of the puzzling questions surrounding the authorship controversy with the evidence decisively supporting the case for Edward de Vere, the 17th Earl of Oxford, as the rightful author of the Shakespeare plays and poems.

♦Whalen, Richard, F, (ed). (2018). *Hamlet: The Oxfordian Shakespeare Series.*
Santa Fe, NM. Horatio Editions.
--With extensive commentary and annotation of the text, Whalen makes it possible to read **Hamlet** *as an autobiography of its author. As one of Edward de Vere's most autobiographical works, the text of the play*

provides an especially rich source of material for annotation from an Oxfordian perspective.

♦Whittemore, Hank. (2016), *100 Reasons Shake-speare Was the Earl of Oxford.*
Somerville MA. Forever Press.
► Also with further discussion and public comment at:
Hank Whittemore's Shakespeare Blog.
        https://hankwhittemore.com/
--In both the book and online blog cited above, Whittemore presents a concise introduction to the authorship question that examines 100 different aspects, from biographical and historical records, that point to Edward de Vere as the true writer of the Shake-speare plays and poems.

Websites & Videos

► De Vere Society. (2019). The de Vere Society – Dedicated to the proposition that the works of Shakespeare were written by Edward de Vere, 17th Earl of Oxford. [online] Deveresociety.co.uk. Available at: https://deveresociety.co.uk
--A very complete resource with substantial biographical and authorship information and links.

► The Oxford Fellowship (2019). Shakespeare Oxford Fellowship | Research and Discussion of the Shakespeare Authorship Question. [online] Shakespeare Oxford Fellowship. Available at: https://shakespeareoxfordfellowship.org/
--A seminal online resource especially focusing on the authorship question.

▶ Waugh, A. (2019). Alexander Waugh. [online] YouTube. Available at: https://www.youtube.com/channel/UCIIN7SCKlsa9lPYJmqqQ2uIg/featured/
OR simply search: 'Alexander Waugh'
--*Alexander Waugh is a leading authorship scholar who has produced many fascinating video presentations on the authorship question. This link is to his YouTube Channel.*

▶ Columbia Pictures & Centropolis Entertainment. (2011). *Anonymous.* Produced and directed by Roland Emmerich. [DVD]
--*This mainstream film is both entertaining and enlightening. It presents a superb dramatization of the character of Edward de Vere, setting out in detail the historical and personal context which made his anonymous authorship necessary.*

▶Centropolis Entertainment and First Folio Pictures. *Last Will and Testament.* (2012). [DVD]
--*A thoughtful and ground-breaking video documentary introduction to the Shakespeare authorship question.*

Acknowledgment
Our sincere thanks to
The de Vere Society
and
The Shakespeare Oxford Fellowship
*for their inspiration, help and support
in creating this series.*

Attributions
*--Character list from Wikipedia under the
Creative Commons License 3.0
--Play text from the Moby(tm) editions
in the public domain*

Photos
Coat of Arms of Edward de Vere
Source: Wikimedia.org
Author: George Baker / Public domain

The Keep at Castle Hedingham
Source: geograph.org.uk
Author: David Phillips / CC BY-SA 2.0

The de Vere Family Coat of Arms
Source: Wikimedia
Author: Rs-nourse / CC BY-SA 3.0
(https://creativecommons.org/licenses/by-sa/3.0)

View from The Minstrels' Gallery, Hedingham Castle
Source: geograph.org.uk/p/3162585
Photo by: © PAUL FARMER - cc-by-sa/2.0

This work has been edited and produced by

Verus Publishing
www.verusbooks.com

V | P

www.ingramcontent.com/pod-product-compliance
Lightning Source LLC
Chambersburg PA
CBHW030417100426
42812CB00028B/2994/J